THE FEAR BUBBLE

BY THE SAME AUTHOR

First Man In

ANT MIDDLETON
THE FEAR BUBBLE

HARNESS FEAR
AND
LIVE WITHOUT LIMITS

HarperCollins*Publishers*

HarperCollins*Publishers*
1 London Bridge Street
London SE1 9GF

www.harpercollins.co.uk

First published by HarperCollins*Publishers* 2019

1 3 5 7 9 10 8 6 4 2

A catalogue record of this book is
available from the British Library

HB ISBN 978-0-00-819466-6
PB ISBN 978-0-00-819467-3

Printed and bound in Great Britain by
CPI Group (UK) Ltd, Croydon

MIX
Paper from
responsible sources
FSC™ C007454

For my wife and children, who have been there for me without fail: Emilie, Oakley, Shyla, Gabriel, Priseïs and Bligh. You give me the driving force to become the best version of myself and to want to succeed at everything I do. You really are my everything. Never forget that.

CONTENTS

CONTENTS

PROLOGUE

THERE WERE TEN of us up there, single file up a narrow track of rock and ice. The going was hard, the incline steep. We'd been up and out of our sleeping bags since dawn, with heavy daypacks strapped to our backs, and were hungry and thirsty and tired. Toes were sore and fingers were numb. The freezing air dried our mouths. I'd never been so high off the ground. The climb was such that we were half-crawling, ankles bent, hands grabbing at anything that looked as if it might take our weight. There wasn't much time to look around and take in the view, but with every glimpse upwards I took I could sense the world getting bluer and bigger around us as the sky swelled into a high dome. With every movement of arm, leg and lung, we were leaving our every-day lives further behind and inching higher into the heavens. It felt rare and unsettling.

The further we climbed, up towards the mountain's famous pyramidal peak, the thinner the track became and the slower the going. Nobody was talking any more. There was no laddy banter or gruff words of encouragement among the men, only grunting and panting and the silence of intense concentration. As I pushed on, I kept reminding myself that we were walking in the steps of my mountaineering hero Edmund Hillary, who'd penetrated these glacial valleys, known hereabouts as 'cwms', and scaled these icy cliffs more than six decades ago. We were way above the birds, it seemed, intruding into the realm of the gods and playing by their rules. I tried not to focus on the height or the danger, although I could feel the fear as a kind of tense sickness in my gut. This was getting serious. A couple of steps to the right and you were off the mountain. Dead.

A crack. A cry.

'Shit!'

A rock the size of a cannonball flew past my face, missing my jaw by about half an inch. It was so close I could smell its cold metallic tang as it shot by. I lurched out of the way, skidding on the track, almost following the rock down. Above my head a brown boot scrabbled on the snowy scree for purchase. I looked down to see the rock being swallowed by the abyss, smacking and echoing as it bashed down the mountainside. An icy wind blew around my neck and face.

'You all right?' I shouted up.

The lad above me was gripping on to the mountainside, as if the earth itself were shaking. His cheeks were pale, his shoulders slumped, his gaze rigid.

'Yeah,' he said. And then, with a little more assurance, 'Yes, mate.'

I watched him steel himself and try swallow his dread. He turned to carry on.

'Good man.'

He lifted his leg once again, trying to find a more secure foothold. But then he paused, his boot hovering mid-air. He sucked in tightly through his chapped lips, breath billowing out.

'I'm coming down,' he said. 'It's, er … I'm, er …'

I thought he was going to lose it. His breathing became rapid and he started looking all around him, as if surrounded by invisible buzzing demons.

'Just take it slow,' I shouted up.

As he picked his way past me, I pressed my body into the freezing incline. His fear was infectious. I wanted so badly to go with him. It was safe down there. There was tea and biscuits and shelter. What the fuck was I doing up here? What was the point? What was I trying to achieve? The mountain didn't want us crawling up it like fleas, it was making that all too obvious. It was trying to shake us off, one by one. Who was I to think I could take it on? Who was I to think I could succeed where Hillary himself had struggled? How was I supposed to know where to put my feet? The guy in front of me had placed his foot on a rock that looked like it had been rooted in place for a thousand years, and it had nearly made him fall off the mountain and taken me with him.

'What you doing, Midsy?' came a frustrated voice from below. 'Come on!'

I had to make a decision, one way or the other. I had to commit. Up? Or down?

Up.

I pushed myself back into a climbing position. The instant my body followed my mind's instruction, something incredible happened. The entire mountain changed. It wasn't trying to shake me off any more – it was pulling me towards it. Every rock had been put there, not to trick me, but to help me. When they worked loose from the mountainside and gave way, that wasn't the mountain trying to kill me, that was the mountain telling me where not to put my feet. These icy gullies weren't death slides, they were ladders. Look how beautiful it was up there. I'd never seen anything like it. I'd never felt anything like I was feeling, right then. I would achieve this. I would fight the fear. I would use it like fuel. I would make it up there, to the top of the world, to the seat of the gods. I would conquer heaven.

CHAPTER 1

TAMING THE GHOST OF ME

Twenty Years Later

'LIGHT?'

'Cheers, buddy.'

I took a few rapid, light puffs of my cigar and heard it crackle into life between my fingers. The smoke that licked the back of my throat was rich and smooth, almost spicy. I took a deeper draw and peered at its glowing end. You could taste that it was expensive. But was this really £400 worth of cigar? That would make it, what, five quid a puff? I settled more deeply into the leather club chair and drew again, this time luxuriating in the experience, allowing the smoke to slide out through my lips gradually and wreathe about my face in silky ribbons. Before it dissipated, I took a sip of the rare single malt whisky my new barrister friend Ivan had also bought me, this time at the bargain price of £60 a shot.

'So, how are you enjoying your new life?' he asked me, his accent as cut-glass as the tumbler in my hand.

His wry expression told me he probably wasn't expecting an answer. After all, wasn't it obvious? To all outward appearances my new life was going brilliantly. I'd seen my face on billboards, and my latest TV show *Mutiny* had been broadcast to millions of viewers and enjoyed critical acclaim. If that wasn't enough, I was in the middle of a sold-out tour of the UK. Every night, in a different town, I'd spend a couple of hours on stage, talking thousands of fans through some of my favourite moments, not just from *Mutiny* but from two series of *SAS: Who Dares Wins*. I'd then be whisked away in a black Mercedes with tinted windows to a five-star hotel where an ice-cold beer and twenty-four-hour room service were waiting for me.

And here I was being wined and dined by a top barrister in one of the most exclusive and secretive private members' clubs in the world. If you've not heard of 5 Hertford Street, it's because the owners like it that way. If you walked past it, you wouldn't know it was there. It's set in a warren of closely packed streets in Shepherd Market, Mayfair, a corner of the capital that used to bristle with high-class vice and scandal but now, aside from a red light bulb or two that shines out of an upstairs window, is polished and prim and postcard perfect. Downstairs, I could hear the faint bass throb of music coming from Loulou's, its nightclub. Next door, the beautiful faces of London high society ate Sicilian prawns or duck with broccoli in the restaurant, their scrubbed and trimmed dogs at their side. This was where billionaires, moguls and the aristocracy of both Hollywood and Britain's most gilded families went for their Friday-night drinks. And tonight I was among them.

'So, you're enjoying it, I take it?' Ivan asked again.

'What's that?' I said.

'Is everything all right, Ant? You're miles away.'

'Oh, sorry, bud,' I smiled. 'Yeah, it's not bad. It's OK. I'm bedding in.'

Ivan was one of the elite. He fitted right in to this place, gliding over the sumptuously patterned carpets and past the heavy, gilt-framed paintings with graceful ease. The fact was, with his blue pinstriped Turnbull & Asser suit, his wide pale yellow tie rakishly unknotted and his long fringe swept back, he'd have fitted right in anywhere in the monied world – London, Singapore, Frankfurt or Dubai.

'Well, yes, I can quite imagine,' he said. 'It must be a rather different experience being entertained here than it was back in the mess.'

'The mess?'

'That's right, isn't it?' He swirled the golden liquid in his glass and absent-mindedly watched the lights dance across its surface. 'In the military. Where you ate. The mess. That is what you call it? I've always thought that rather odd.'

'Why odd?'

'Well, it's a joke, I take it. Irony. Military humour.' His eyes flicked up. 'I mean, you know, *are* they messy places? One would rather imagine not.'

Between us there was a small mahogany table on which sat a heavy, polished-iron ashtray in the shape of a leaf. I tapped my cigar onto its edge and found myself mentally weighing it. It was big. Hefty.

'It's French,' I told him. 'From the word *"mets"*, meaning a dish or a portion of food. It's not because it's ...'

'Oh, is that so!' he said, laughing. 'Of course. Yes, I should have known. Yes, yes, how silly of me. The French.' He kind of half-winked in my direction. 'That was an impressive stab at a French accent there, by the way, Ant. It felt, just for a moment, as if I'd been whisked away to the harbour at St Tropez.'

Yeah, that ashtray had to weigh a good three or four kilos. Maybe more. You could do some proper damage with that. Put a door in. In fact, you could put someone's head in with that thing. Easily. I'd use the bottom edge. Curl my fingers into the bowl, get some proper purchase on it and wear it like a knuckle-duster. *Wallop.*

'I grew up in France, as it happens,' I told him.

'In France? Well, I never. Whereabouts?'

'So I'm fluent in French.'

'Well, bravo,' he said, raising his glass. 'Cheers to you. And I do hope we can come to some arrangement over this company retreat in April. We'll fly you in first-class. It would be a real morale booster for the firm to have you come along and speak to the troops, even if they're not of quite the same physical calibre as the troops you're used to working with. Although, saying that, some of the chaps and chapesses in the office are terribly into the fitness scene – it's quite impossible to get them out of the gym at lunchtimes. But it gets harder as you get older, doesn't it? I expect this new phase of your career has come at just the right time for you. Even if you do miss the military life, when you get to our age, it's … I mean, you're clearly in very fine shape. I try to keep in reasonably decent order myself. But the selection process. The SAS. Do people our age do it? People in their forties?'

'Ivan, mate, I'm thirty-seven,' I said.

'Of course you are. I'm so sorry. I didn't mean to imply … Of course you could still pass Selection. You'd fly through it. You've only got to see your television programmes …' He was beginning to bluster.

'Ivan, mate, it's totally fine,' I said, laughing. 'Forget it. Fucking forties! What are you like?'

As he relaxed once again, he began telling me about his own fitness regime. No carbs after 6 p.m., forty-five minutes in his home gym three times a week, a personal trainer called Samson. As I listened, enjoying my cigar, I found myself beginning to wonder, what would happen if it all kicked off in a place like this? What if Isis came through the door? A lone shooter or a guy in a bomb vest? What would Ivan do? How would that waiter over there respond? Rugby tackle him? Go for his legs? Or shit himself and dive under the table? I scanned the people around me. They'd go into a flat panic. Every single one of them.

I know what I'd do. I'd head-dive into cover, down there in the corner, and then I'd come around and try to disarm him. I'd use the ashtray as a weapon. I'd crack it right over him. Right around the fucking face. Smack. Cave in his cheekbone and then go straight into a backswing, push his chin up into his nose. God, I would love to see it kick off in here. That old geezer in the corner in the bow tie just turning around head-butting that fat dude with the pink hanky in his top pocket – landing it perfectly between the eyes, knocking the cunt into the fire. That woman in the lily dress giving the terrorist a proper crack in the jaw, bursting his nose open with that massive jewel on her finger. Some old Duke being kicked down the stairs by a minor royal in stilettos. Yes. *Yes!* What would it take for this place to go up? I would pay good money to see that.

'To success!' said Ivan. Suddenly, I was back in my body. The room instantly reorganised itself back into its hushed, murmuring and peaceful state. There was no blood on the walls or scalp on the carpet. The stairs were empty of violence. I was no longer crouched on that £10,000 rug de-braining a terrorist.

'Success!' I replied.

I raised my glass and downed it all.

SUCCESS. IS THIS what it was? Warm rooms and expensive dinners? Small talk with top barristers about personal fitness and fat cheques for corporate events? An hour later, as I strode down to Green Park tube past pubs and art galleries and dark human forms hurrying along the wet pavements, I found myself brooding. When I left the Special Forces in 2011, I had no idea what I was going to do with the rest of my life. What could I possibly achieve that would be better than the buzz of leading a Hard Arrest Team in the badlands of various war zones over two intensely frightening and violent tours of duty? Life back home in Chelmsford, I quickly discovered, was not like life in Helmand Province. I found it difficult to adjust, ending up physically assaulting a police officer and serving time in prison. The easiest thing I could have done, when I hit those lows, was to join my friends and associates in their criminal gangs. It wasn't as if they hadn't tried hard and repeatedly to recruit me. Someone with my background, I knew, had enormous value to those kinds of organisations – and I'd be handsomely rewarded. I would certainly have ended up wealthier than I was now. And the excitement? Oh, that would have been there, no doubt about it.

As I reached the end of the dark, narrow corridor of White Horse Road, a young couple were walking in my direction. The girl, her pale face framed in a white parka hood, gave a slight double-take when she saw me. I hunched my shoulders and sent my gaze to the floor. Please don't ask for a selfie. Not now. When they were safely in the distance I went to cross the road and waited at the kerb. The usually busy lanes of Piccadilly were at a rare lull. I looked left and then right. There were a couple of double-decker buses, one coming in each direction, both trailing a stream of taxis and vans behind them. I waited. And then I waited some more, allowing them to get even closer. At the final instant, just as they were about to roar past my face, I darted out, dodging one and then the other, feeling their fumes billow around me as I danced between them.

I knew only too well why so many former Special Forces operators ended up either on the street, traumatised and addicted, or working for a criminal firm. Because success in civilian life lacks something that we've come to crave. You can't take it out of us. It's in there for life. And it's not the fault of the military training, either. You can't blame that. The fact is, we're simply those kinds of men. We exist on that knife edge. Go one way, they'll end up calling you a hero, a protector of the public and the nation. Go just a little in the other direction and you'll find yourself in prison, an enemy of the same public and the same nation. The extreme forms of training that admittance into the Special Forces demands don't *cause* us to be these kinds of people. It just takes what's already there, hones it, draws it out and teaches us to control it. The problem is, this quality doesn't simply evaporate when you leave the SAS or, in my case, the SBS. It's still in there. It's in your blood. It's in your daydreams. It's in how you walk. It's in the way you scan a room the moment you enter it, looking for entry and escape routes, pockets of cover and potential aggressors.

And it's also in how you cross the road. I'd noticed myself doing that increasingly over the last few weeks. If I was in

London, or in one of the traffic-choked streets in the centre of Chelmsford, and I saw a pedestrian crossing with the green man flashing, I wouldn't run to catch it like everyone else. I'd slow down. I'd wait until the traffic was fast and raging again, and only then would I cross. I'd never do this in front of my wife Emilie and certainly not in front of my kids. To be honest, I was only half-conscious of doing it myself. I hardly even knew how to explain it, apart from to say that it was that edge I was after, that edge I would go looking for anywhere – a brief moment of danger to keep my heart beating and my spirit alive. That threat, that trouble, that fear. I was constantly looking for opportunities to push myself, test myself and add a little dose of risk to my otherwise overwhelmingly safe days.

So that was it. That was why Ivan had provoked a host of strange and uncomfortable emotions to come bubbling out from deep within me when he'd asked if I was enjoying what he called my 'new life'. Of course I enjoyed its trappings. Who wouldn't? It felt great to achieve so much in these areas of popular culture that I'd never have even dreamed of entering just a few years ago. You couldn't deny I was successful. But this wasn't my kind of success. I felt as if I were somehow losing my identity. And the problem was, my identity was beginning to fight back. I could feel it punching and kicking, whenever I was in meetings with guys like Ivan or in places like 5 Hertford Street. The warrior inside me would rise out of nowhere and take over my thoughts. I'd find myself daydreaming about terrorist attacks or mass brawls breaking out, building my strategy for dealing with the madness, assessing everyone around me in terms of how much of a threat they'd be and how I could take them out. This could happen to me anywhere – in the ground-floor canteen at Channel 4 or on the set of *This Morning*, waiting to be interviewed by Phil and Holly in front of millions of viewers. It was like I was being possessed by the ghost of the man who used to be me. And the really worrying thing was, these weren't waking nightmares that left me in cold sweats. They weren't PTSD-like moments of dread and horror. They were fantasies. I was willing them to happen.

After the deep orange darkness of London's November streets, the lights inside Green Park tube station felt too bright, and I squinted a little as I ran down the long flights of stairs towards my platform, racing the people descending the escalators on either side of me. I found a quiet seat at the end of a carriage and jammed my hands into the pockets of my jacket. A few seats away from me a couple of girls sat opposite each other. They looked to be in their early twenties, and were giggling and laughing in that drunk schoolgirl way. One had taken her high heels off, and her bare toes were now blackened from the tube floor. An unopened bottle of WKD Red stuck out of her lime-green handbag. Another, open and half drunk, was clutched in her hands. The other girl wore a tight white mini-dress and had a tattoo of Michael Jackson on her arm. Her faux leather jacket lay on the seat beside her, along with their crumpled Burger King wrappers and boxes.

When I stepped into the carriage they'd been cackling loudly, but once they clocked me they fell into a hushed chatter, interspersed by periodic piggy, nasal snorts of laughter.

'Here we go,' I thought. 'I've been spotted.' But then I checked myself. Maybe not. One of the things about finding yourself unexpectedly well known – among certain parts of the general public, at least – is that it's easy to become paranoid. You start to think that everyone's watching you, wherever you go, even though most members of the public would never have even heard of you. Anyone who's been on the TV for more than ten minutes has an embarrassing story to tell about a stranger coming up to them in the street, and them presenting their finest prime-time Saturday-night smile and preparing to quickly scribble out an autograph, only for that person to ask if they know the directions to the nearest McDonald's.

The girls were now leaning into each other and whispering intensely. I wondered what they were they doing. Plotting their next assassination? I kept noticing their eyes swivelling out from their dark huddle and looking in my direction. Then they abruptly sat back, now not saying anything. Suddenly a phone appeared. It was in a black case with Michael Jackson picked out in fake diamonds, one hand on his trilby, the other on his crotch. The girl in the mini-dress was holding it directly in front of her face, but some distance away from her, like an old lady squinting at a book. Then it turned slowly in my direction. The girl looked upwards, now apparently closely examining the advert for student home insurance above the window opposite her. There was the faint electronic sound of a shutter being clicked. Her mate snorted with laughter. 'Shut up!' the first one hissed.

I wouldn't mind if they'd asked. I never complain about being recognised or having to pose for selfies, as that would be ungrateful and disrespectful. And I'd hate – more than anything – to be perceived as being rude to anyone. Having said that, I always try to keep my head down when I'm out and about. I never pretend that I'm someone. I hate being in that mindset, thinking that I'm the centre of attention. But more and more, things like this kept happening. I'd leave the house and be reminded very quickly that my existence had changed. There wasn't much I could do about it. This was the reality of the 'new life' that Ivan had been asking about.

It was a life that didn't come without its own peculiar risks. I only had to walk out of a pub looking unsteady and some newspaper somewhere would print a story that I was an alcoholic. I only had to scowl in someone's direction and it would be reported that I was in the middle of a heated argument. So I needed to make sure that my behaviour in public wasn't merely immaculate – it could never even be *perceived* to be anything less than immaculate, even down to the expression on my face.

Maintaining that level of good behaviour wasn't easy, especially for someone with a past like mine. It wasn't a comfortable combination, all those eyeballs, all that stress – and my personality. The more I felt watched, the more that old, raucous version of me wanted to kick back. The intense pressure to behave immaculately – in trains, on the street and within private members' clubs – taunted that unstable ghost living inside me. It goaded him and mocked him and motivated him to take me over. I felt him writhing around, pushing at me, tempting me to make chaos. As the girl took another photo, and this time barely bothered to pretend she wasn't, I buried my fists deeper into my pockets and pushed my chin into the collar of my coat, as my left leg bounced up and down in nervous, aggravated motion. 'I should've got a car back,' I thought to myself. 'Fuck this. I'm not taking the tube any more. I'm going to stop taking public transport.'

By the time I got to Liverpool Street station I'd done a lot of serious reflecting. What on earth was I thinking? Who was I turning into? Some TV celebrity puffing on £400 cigars who refuses to go on the underground? In that moment with the girls and the photos, it felt as if everything I was, everything I'd fought so hard to become, was at risk of getting lost. I didn't want to fall head first into this new life, with its new definition of success. It wasn't just that I was worried I'd change for the worse and become some spoiled 'celebrity'. I was afraid that if I didn't grab hold of the situation, the old me would fight back in a way that I couldn't control. There was a genuine danger that I would revert to finding my buzzes elsewhere. That could be drinking. That could be fighting. That could be getting myself killed by a double-decker bus. Too many people were relying on me these days for that to happen. It wasn't only my wife and five children. My life had somehow turned into a small industry. There were teams of people making serious parts of their livelihoods off the back of me, and all of them needed me out of prison and off the tabloid scandal pages, not underneath ten tonnes of steel and rubber in the middle of Piccadilly. My success and theirs were intertwined. I felt a responsibility to every single one of them.

But what could I do? How could I exorcise this ghost when I had all these eyeballs on me? Perhaps I could take a spell out of the limelight and go back to West Africa, where I'd carried out some security work before life in the media found me. That might be fun – I'd get into some interesting scrapes – but there was no way I'd get it past Emilie. It was too sketchy. I thought about running a marathon or taking up boxing in a serious way, but neither of these would really test me. I needed that perfect balance, somewhere I could feel fear but actually be relatively safe.

As soon as I had that thought, an incredibly vivid memory came to me. It was so powerful it was like being in a momentary dream, one that took me back all of twenty years, when I was seventeen. It was my first adventure training package in the army, and we'd climbed Snowdon in Wales. Before that day, during basic training, my life in the military had been extremely controlled. We'd been spit-polishing boots, doing drills and press-ups and running around in the mud, all under the instruction of barking troop sergeants, with almost every minute of every day being tightly regimented. Even though I'd been pushed to my limits, it had all been done in an environment of safety. I'd been scared and intimidated, but the only things I'd really had to fear were failure and humiliation – threats to my feelings. It had been fake danger. And then we'd climbed the mountain.

And it wasn't just any mountain. It was Snowdon, at 3,560 feet the highest peak in England and Wales. It was said to be where Sir Edmund Hillary himself had trained for his successful assault on Mount Everest. When we reached the summit that day I remember thinking, 'Fucking hell, I've just climbed a mountain!' It felt like the greatest achievement of my life. I'd never experienced getting out into the world like that before. I'd never felt as if I'd truly conquered anything. And there I was, on top of the world, breathing the air of the gods.

But that wasn't the only reason my memory of Snowdon was so precious. After my father suddenly died at the age of just 36, on 31 December 1985, my mum and her young boyfriend Dean moved the family from our three-bedroom council house in Portsmouth first to an eight-bedroom mansion outside Southampton, and then to northern France. Flush with money from my dad's life-insurance payout, they bought a huge house that had once been a children's home on a large plot of land on the outskirts of a town called Saint-Lô, twenty miles from Bayeux. Life with my mother and new step-father was tough, and my happiest times were the hours I'd spend tearing around in the fields and woods playing soldiers. I had a wild time, and even at that age I began to wonder about being an actual soldier when I was older.

As wild as those days had felt to me, however, they had really been lived within a controlled environment. Even when I stayed in one of my dens for two or three nights, someone would always have to know where I was. If I ever got into trouble I'd feel it. Part of why I wanted to join the army was my urge to re-create those experiences of wild adventure under open skies. But in the early weeks and months after I joined up, the experience had been more like being at home with my stepfather. I was always watched and pushed and corrected by a figure of authority.

All of that changed on my ascent of Snowdon. My most vivid memory of all, even more than of reaching the top, was when I saw the lad in front of me almost fall off a narrow track, right off the side of it. I'd seen the fear first grip him, then overwhelm him, and watched him give up the climb completely, fumbling his way back down to safety. I'd become infected with that same fear. It had soaked into me like a heavy, disabling liquid. I looked around me and real-ised I was on the edge of death. Anything could have gone wrong. I could have slipped. The weather could have come in. I could have got hypothermia or been blown off the mountain. I'd never experienced such vulnerability. For the first time, I felt that I had my own life in my hands. As the fear washed through me I had to make that decision. Do I listen to what it's telling me? Or do I trust myself to do this? Do I go up? Or down?

It was that *fear* I remembered most. As I paced up and down the platform at Liverpool Street waiting for the Chelmsford train I was in a trance of memory, feeling it again as if it was all happening to me right now. That fear had almost beaten me. But the moment I'd committed to the decision to climb, an incredible transformation had taken place. My perception changed. It had been as if the mountain itself had stopped trying to hurl me down its precipitous flanks. Now, instead, it was drawing me up to its summit and I no longer felt as if I were on the edge of death.

Why had that change occurred? How had it happened? Partly, I realised, it was because, in making the decision to continue on upwards, I'd fully embraced the responsibility of my task. There were no rules on that mountain except for the ones I gave myself. There was no drill instructor telling me where to look or put my feet. There was no stepfather telling me what time I had to be in or where I could or couldn't go. It was lawless up there. Amid the freezing blasts of wind I found an ecstatic sense of liberation on Snowdon that was completely new to me. I was in real danger on that narrow, icy track. If I made the wrong decision it was entirely down to me, and I alone would pay the price. That was petrifying. But it was also exciting. I was my own god up there. I felt completely alive in a way that I never had done before. I felt afraid – and I felt free.

I found a quiet seat on the train where no stray eyeballs or selfie cameras were likely to find me and excitedly pulled my phone out of my pocket. How long did it take to drive to Snowdon? I'd go up it again. Do it solo. The next weekend I had free. That's it, it was decided. I wondered if I could remember the exact route we'd taken twenty years ago. It wasn't one of the normal tourist routes. It was … I didn't know. Well, what was the toughest way up? I opened up my web browser and typed in S.N.O. … I stopped. Snowdon? Really? I was seventeen when I'd done it. I was thirty-seven now, and a completely different man. I could walk up Snowdon in silk slippers. It just wouldn't do. It wouldn't give me what I needed. So what would? What's the ultimate Snowdon? I went back to the web browser on my phone and deleted S.N.O. … In the place of those letters, I pecked out a new word.

E.V.E.R.E.S.T.

As the train wobbled to a start and began to rattle out of the station towards home, I excitedly scanned the results on Google. One page leapt out at me. A Wikipedia article: 'List of people who died climbing Mount Everest'. I began reading.

Mount Everest, at 8,848 metres (29,029 ft), is the world's highest mountain and a particularly desirable peak for mountaineers. Over 290 people have died trying to climb it. The last year without known deaths on the mountain was 1977, a year in which only two people reached the summit.

Most deaths have been attributed to avalanches, injury from fall, serac collapse, exposure, frostbite or health problems related to conditions on the mountain. Not all bodies have been located, so details on those deaths are not available.

The upper reaches of the mountain are in the death zone. The 'death zone' is a mountaineering term for altitudes above a certain point – around 8,000 m (26,000 ft), or less than 356 millibars (5.16 psi) of atmospheric pressure – where the oxygen level is not sufficient to sustain human life. Many deaths in high-altitude mountaineering have been caused by the effects of the death zone, either directly (loss of vital functions) or indirectly (unwise decisions made under stress or physical weakening leading to accidents). In the death zone, the human body cannot acclimatise, as it uses oxygen faster than it can be replenished. An extended stay in the zone without supplementary oxygen will result in deterioration of bodily functions, loss of consciousness and, ultimately, death.

Why did people die on the mountain every year? There must be something special up there. And what was this 'death zone' they were going on about? What did a death zone actually look like? What would it feel like to tackle one? It sounded as if you only got a certain amount of time to climb the mountain before you ran out of oxygen – that climbers used 'oxygen faster than it can be replenished'. So it was like a race for your life. I felt my heart lurch with excitement. I scrolled down the page to the seemingly endless list of fatalities. The deaths started with the very first expedition to attempt to climb the mountain, undertaken by a British team in 1922. Seven Nepalese guys, who I guessed were helping them get to the top, died on the same day in an avalanche. Two years later, there was a Brit, Andrew Irvine: 'Disappeared; body never found; cause of death unknown'. He was twenty-two. With him, another Brit, the famous George Mallory. 'Disappeared; body found in 1999; evidence suggests Mallory died from being accidentally struck by his ice axe following a fall.'

As I kept scrolling, the deaths mounted up. Wang Ji, China, 1960, 'mountain sickness'; Harsh Vardhan Bahuguna, India, 1971, 'succumbed after falling and being suspended above a crevasse during a blizzard'; Mario Piana, Italy, 1980, 'crushed under serac'. My eyes flicked across to the column that noted the causes of death. There were hundreds of entries, page after page: avalanche, avalanche, fall, fall, exposure, exposure, exposure, drowning, heart attack, high-altitude pulmonary oedema (HAPE), high-altitude cerebral oedema (HACE), exhaustion, organ failure due to freezing conditions. And these people were from all over the planet: Australia, Germany, Taiwan, Canada, Bulgaria, South Korea, the United States, Vietnam, Switzerland … Finally, I reached the end of the list. 2017. This year. Six deaths. An Indian, a Slovakian, an Australian, an American, a Nepalese and a Swiss guy. Causes of death? Everything from altitude sickness to 'fall into a 200m crevasse'.

Of all the names I'd seen on that page, I'd only heard of one: George Mallory. I knew, of course, that Hillary had been the first man in, up on Everest's summit, but why was Mallory so famous? I clicked on his name and began reading the article about him. It turned out that he'd taken part in the first three expeditions to the mountain, the first a reconnaissance expedition in 1921, the second two being serious attempts to ascend the peak in 1922 and 1924. He was last seen alive just 245 feet away from the summit, and it remains unknown whether he reached the top before his death. He'd served in the military, as a second lieutenant in the Royal Garrison Artillery, and fought at the Battle of the Somme. I noticed his age on the day he died.

Thirty-seven.

* * *

'BUT ANT, YOU said *Mutiny* was your last thing.'

It was the following morning, just after 7.30 a.m., and I was disappointed to discover that 5 Hertford Street £60-a-shot whisky gives you exactly the same hangovers as the stuff from Tesco at £6.99 a bottle. My wife Emilie was at the counter with her back to me, preparing breakfast for our one-year-old boy. I'd forgotten I'd made that promise to her. But she was right. *Mutiny*, the TV show I'd filmed the previous year, re-created the 4,000-mile journey across the Pacific Ocean in a twenty-three-foot wooden boat undertaken by Captain Bligh and eighteen crewmen following the mutiny on HMS *Bounty* in 1789. That had been a tougher-than-expected sell when I'd first run it past her. Looking back, the idea was borderline insane. Together with the nine men I was responsible for, we'd braved wild storms, twenty-foot waves, starvation, dehydration and the onset of madness, and I'd only just made it back in time for the birth of the amazing boy – named Bligh – whom Emilie was now spooning mashed bananas into.

'Well, I actually said *Mutiny* was the last *stupid* thing I'd do,' I told her. 'Everest isn't stupid. Hundreds of people do it every year. It's just a holiday, really. A camping trip.'

'And how long will you be gone on this camping trip?'

'Er, it takes about six weeks, give or take.'

'Six weeks?'

'Yeah, because you need to acclimatise. The air up the mountain is so thin you've got to give your body a chance to get used to it. So you go up a little way, rest and get used to the altitude, then you go down, rest some more, and then you go up again, but a bit higher.'

'Sounds annoying.'

She was still in her pyjamas and had her hair pulled back in a loose ponytail. I often think of the word 'angelic' when I see Emilie. She has a perfect, heart-shaped face – her cheekbones are wide and high, and her chin forms the cutest little bump. Her eyes are large and dark green, speckled with brown that sometimes, in the right light, seems to glisten like pale gold. She has exactly the kind of face you'd imagine on an angel.

'It's just being careful,' I told her. 'It's the safest way of doing things.'

I took the spoon off her and began feeding Bligh myself.

'I'm not up for taking any risks up there, babes. This isn't for a TV show or anything, so there'll be no drama. It's just a bit of fun. An old pal of mine from the military takes people up there every year. He's got a company that does it. Proper professional outfit. Here you go …'

I unlocked my phone. The website of my friend's organisation, Elite Himalayan Adventures, was still on my web browser from when I'd last looked at it. I passed it over to her and she picked it up warily. I'd spent the rest of my train journey the previous night reading pretty much every page of it. Elite Himalayan Adventures specialised in expeditions up the world's fourteen highest mountains including

Kangchenjunga on the border of Nepal and Sikkim, K2 in Pakistan, and the king of them all, Mount Everest. The page I showed Emilie highlighted the company's emphasis on not putting their clients in any undue danger: 'Safety will always be our priority, and all of our Sherpa guides are expert climbers and expedition leaders in their own right, who then undergo a rigorous selection and training process to ensure you get the safest, most informed and most professional climbing experience possible.'

'Looks fun.' She put the phone down and started noisily unloading the dishwasher. 'But six weeks, Ant?'

'Well, the entire trip, with actually getting to the mountain in the first place ... I mean, you're probably talking more like two months, if I'm honest.'

'And how much is this two-month holiday going to cost?' she said, over the sound of bowls being stacked in the cupboard.

'It's not exactly cheap. But we're doing OK, aren't we? I've been working hard.'

'I know, Ant,' she said, still not looking at me. 'You have. It's totally up to you. What are we talking, though? For the trip?'

'It's probably ... I don't know.' I did know. 'Sixty grand? Give or take?'

There was a silence. I watched her put a pile of plates down, slowly and gently on the counter, and then pull a chair out opposite me.

'This isn't a wind-up, is it?' she said in disbelief once she'd sat down. 'I can tell by your face it's not a wind-up.'

I spooned another mouthful of banana into Bligh.

'It's just what it costs, babe.'

'But why does it cost sixty grand?' she said. 'I mean, sixty grand? For a camping trip? How did they work that one out?'

'Emilie, you've got to trust me. I need to get away. This new life we're building is great but I'm beginning to feel claustrophobic. I keep having these thoughts. It's hard to explain.'

I put the sticky spoon down and looked her in the eye.

'I don't want to muck anything up for us. I don't want to do anything stupid. If I manage to behave myself, it's just onwards and upwards for us and the kids. There'll be no stopping us. But there's a lot of steam building up. I can feel it. And if I don't let it off up that mountain, I might end up doing it outside some bar or something. If I don't get the buzz I need, I'm going to find that buzz myself, whether it's breaking the law or offending someone or fighting someone. I can't end up back in that place again. We'd lose everything. It *is* sixty grand. But you should see it as an insurance payment.'

'It's not dangerous, is it?'

'Not for me it isn't. I could walk up Everest backwards. They've had all sorts up there on the summit. Postmen.

Celebrities. It's just an adventure holiday. Just something to sort my head out.'

To be honest, there was never really any chance of Emilie standing in the way of my going. Although she sometimes worried about me, she always trusted me, and I always respected her enough to run anything I wanted to do past her. When I'd served in the military, she hadn't been like the wives and girlfriends of some of the other men, worrying and fussing and distracting them with the anxieties and problems of home life. As had been my wish, Emilie just let me get on with serving my country when I went away, and that allowed me to keep my head clear and focused on the job in hand. She didn't call. She didn't write letters. And that's exactly how I liked it. Her strength of character helped keep me alive. I'm not exaggerating when I say that Emilie has always been the perfect partner for me. We instinctively understand what each other needs and we always do our best to provide it. Me and her are an unbreakable team.

She also knew I wasn't lying when I told her I could walk up the mountain backwards. In Everest I'd found the ideal challenge to tame that warrior ghost inside me, at least for the time being. Nobody could deny that climbing the world's highest mountain was dangerous. Its list of confirmed kills was impressive. But I wasn't just anyone.

I'd often told Emilie that I was invincible, and I wasn't really joking. I didn't really believe anything could kill me – and it was this belief that had kept me in one piece.

Nothing that had ever been thrown at me had taken me out. All those people I'd read about on Wikipedia who'd fallen down crevasses or succumbed to exhaustion or organ failure or a cerebral oedema, whatever that was – I felt bad for them, but they weren't me. Everest would give me a taste of the danger that I'd begun to crave, that was probably true, but it wasn't going to pose me any genuine problems. If anything, it would be too easy. This would be a camping trip. A walk in the park.

'Thanks, Emilie,' I said, lifting Bligh out of his seat and cradling him against my shoulder. 'I'll get it booked.'

A sudden wave of excitement washed over me and I grinned in her direction.

'How good is it going to be, standing on top of the world?'

CHAPTER 2

HOW TO HARNESS FEAR

WHY DID I want to climb Mount Everest so badly? Why was I taking deliberate, crazy risks when crossing busy roads? Why was my mind slipping into violent fantasies at the very moment I was being made to feel most coddled, in a Mayfair private members' club over expensive whisky and cigars? What kind of a man would imagine such horrific things? Believe me, I didn't want a terrorist to come bursting in with an AK47 and a bomb vest because I'm some psychopath. I didn't want people to get hurt. What I wanted was to be handed a reason to leap up and stop people being hurt. I wanted to be forced into action. I wanted to be put in a position in which I had no choice but to perform or die. What I wanted – what I'd started craving almost like a drug – was fear.

This might seem strange, but that's what my relationship with fear is like. I crave it. I need it. And as much as I need it, I also dread it. As I travel up and down the country meeting people on my tours, one of the questions I always get asked is a variation on this – 'How did you get to be so fearless?' The answer is, I didn't become fearless. I don't believe that's even possible. I feel fear all the time. Not only do I feel it all the time, I hate it. It's not that I've learned to conquer fear or enjoy it. It's that I've learned how to use it. My experiences fighting in Afghanistan with the Marines and serving as 'point man' as a member of the Special Boat Service, the first man in as part of an elite team that was charged with capturing some of the world's most dangerous men, taught me that fear is like a wild horse. You can let it trample all over you, or you can put a harness on it and let it carry you forwards, blasting you unscathed through the finish line.

More than anything else, I believe that my ability to harness fear and use it to my advantage is the secret of my success. There's no way I would have come out of Afghanistan, or any other theatre of war, in a healthy psychological state if I hadn't learned how to do this. And more than that, there's no way I'd have been a success in my personal or professional life if I hadn't developed the ability to grab hold of the incredible power of human fear and let it take me where I wanted to go. I've now got to a place where I rely on fear. When it goes missing from my life I find myself becoming anxious and dissatisfied. Without fear, there's no challenge. Without challenge, there's no growth. Without growth, there's no life.

INTO THE BUBBLE

This method for harnessing fear has changed my life in ways that are almost unimaginable. It's transformed me from the naïve, angry and dangerous young man I once was to the person I am today. The good news is that anyone can learn it. I call it the 'the fear bubble'.

Back when I was in the military, there were many times in the breaks between tours when I caught myself thinking that I didn't want to return. The fear you experience on the battlefield is unbelievably intense. There are many different levels of fear, but 'life or death' is surely the worst of them all. Most people never experience the feeling that when they step around the next corner there's a decent chance they'll take a bullet in the skull. I had to deal with that time and time again.

Many amazingly brave and tough operators didn't find a way of processing that level of fear and horror. I've seen the hardest and best soldiers brought to their knees, reduced to crumbling, quivering wrecks, in floods of tears. That's what fear can do to you if you fail to harness it and let it trample you. Today, many of these men are suffering from serious, debilitating mental disorders from which they might never recover. Their marriages have fallen to pieces, they can't sustain regular employment, and they're utterly lost in drugs and alcohol. Some are homeless, some enmeshed in a life of street crime. They've been destroyed by fear.

Although I was determined not to become one of these men when I served with the military, I could feel the effects of fear creeping up on me. When I was in the Special Forces, I'd be dropped off in a war zone in some grim and dusty back-end of the planet, and then for six interminable months it would feel as if I were utterly trapped in this enormous bubble of constant, crushing dread. As soon as I left the theatre of operations and my plane touched down in the UK, the bubble would suddenly burst and life would be great again. But when I began counting down the days until the start of the next tour, I started to experience that gut-wrenching feeling all over again. I didn't want to go back.

For a while I couldn't work it out. What was wrong with me? What was that heavy, greasy sensation in the pit of my stomach? I loved my job. So why was I feeling that I didn't want to go back? I had to be brutally honest with myself. The truth was, I was shit scared. Fear had got a grip of me, just like it had got a grip of thousands of brave and capable men before me.

I didn't know what to do. How could I ever solve the problem of experiencing intense fear on the battlefield? Of course you're going to be scared when the air is filled with bullets and the ground is filled with IEDs (improvised explosive devices). Surely this was an impossible task? It then occurred to me that if I couldn't get rid of fear completely, perhaps I could break it down into smaller packets so that it was a little less all-consuming and relentless. So that's what I did. After giving it some thought, I realised I needed to adopt a coldly rational view of why I was feeling scared and, even more importantly, *when* I was feeling scared. Why, for example, was I experiencing such dread two weeks before my deployment, when I was still in the safety and joyfulness of my family home? There was nothing to be scared of there. Nothing whatsoever.

And while I was at it, what was the point of being scared when I landed in whatever unnamed conflict zone to which I happened to have been assigned? We were usually stationed in a secure area inside some form of military base. If you actually thought about it, a military base was one of the safest places on the planet, teeming with highly trained men and women, and guarded with the latest military equipment. There was not much, realistically, to be scared about there. Statistically, you were probably more likely to be walking around with an undiagnosed tumour in your body than you were to be killed by the enemy in a place like that, and nobody on the base was running around all day fretting about whether or not they had cancer.

And what about when I was on an actual operation? When I was dropped off behind enemy lines, I didn't need to be in that bubble of fear. No bullets would be flying. We'd land in a safe space and be entirely incognito. The lads would be with me. When I was approaching the target location, where we'd often be attempting the hard arrest of a terrorist leader, there was no point being in that bubble of fear either. That would be a lengthy walk in complete silence through the darkness – several hours of relative safety. It was only when I actually got onto target, where the bad guys were, that it was really appropriate to feel scared.

From my very next mission onwards I put this coldly rational approach to fear into practice. I tried to make it a cast-iron rule. The proper time to feel scared was when we were inside the process of an active operation. At all other times, I told myself, the fear was irrational. Pointless. So shake it off.

And it worked. Kind of. As soon as we hit the target, the fear would take me. I'd be inside that bubble, gripped with absolutely gut-wrenching dread until we were done. After the completion of the mission I'd run on to the helicopter, and the moment the door had closed and we'd lifted off to a safe altitude I'd be out of the bubble. Happy. Elated. Delirious. Thank God. And I wouldn't allow myself to feel fear again until the next mission was in play.

But after a couple of months of this the old feeling started to return. As much as I genuinely loved being a Special Forces operator, the grinding, bubbling sensation in the pit of my stomach when I thought about getting on that helicopter came back. Brutal honesty. I was shit scared. Again.

Although I'd managed to break the fear down into a much smaller and more rational chunk, I realised that even that was too much for me to handle. An active operation could last many hours – and sometimes stretch into days, depending on how bad the situation became. That was too long to spend inside a fear bubble.

The next step was obvious. I'd have to break it down into even smaller packets. From now on, I told myself, I would be absolutely rational and clear-headed about when it was appropriate to feel fear and when it wasn't. Even when I was standing right in front of the terrorist's compound, I decided, I didn't need to be in that bubble. After all, he was probably fast asleep with his thumb in his mouth and his dick in his hand, and his guards would most likely be completely unaware of our presence. So what was the point of feeling fear? There was nothing to be scared of. I was a ghost, at that moment, as invisible as a subtle change in the breeze. It was only when I was under a direct threat – when I knew, for example, that there was a sentry position or an armed guard behind a corner or a door that I was stacked right up against – that it was actually appropriate to feel fear. That precise moment before the bullets flew. That was the time.

It was on the next operation that I had my huge breakthrough. We'd entered a terrorist compound at just gone four in the morning. I knew there was an armed combatant just around the corner of a mud and rock wall that I was approaching. I could see the smoke from his cigarette and the black steel barrel-tip of his AK47 in the green static blur of my night-vision goggles. I looked at the corner and told myself, 'That is where the fear bubble is.' And then I did something new. I visualised the bubble. I could actually see the fear, right there at the place where my life would be in danger. Not where I was standing, ten metres away from it, but over there where the threat actually, truly was. And nor was that fear happening right now, at this moment. I would feel it a few seconds later, when I made the conscious decision to go over there and step into the bubble.

That visualisation changed everything. Fear was no longer a vague, fuzzy concept with the power to utterly overwhelm me like an endless storm. Fear was a place. And fear was a time. That place was not here. And that time was not now. It was over there. I could see it. Shimmering and glinting and throbbing and grinding, and waiting patiently for my arrival.

Now all I had to do was step into it. I girded myself with a deep breath. And then I took a few paces forwards and walked into it. There it was. Fuck. The fear hit me like wave. I was so close to the enemy combatant I could practically smell the stale camel milk on his breath. Now I was in the bubble, I had to act. I made the conscious decision to do what needed to be done.

The moment he hit the dirt, my fear bubble burst. I stepped forward, around the body, as the relief and elation that I was actually still alive ripped through me. Gathering myself together, I saw that I was now in a wider courtyard area. Out of the corner of my eye I glimpsed someone running into a doorway, slamming the door behind him. I felt a sudden surge of fear and then squashed it dead. 'I'm now in this courtyard alone,' I thought to myself. 'There's no danger in this physical location or at this precise time. I'm good. Right now, in this place, at this moment, I'm safe.'

I looked at the door. Behind it lay the enemy. Behind it lay the danger. I visualised the bubble right outside it. I approached the bubble. I took a deep breath. I stepped into it and felt the wave of dread slam into me. I composed myself. Kicked the door down. Entered. Cleared the room. And I was out of the bubble again. And that's how the entire operation continued. When the next target was coming up, I visualised the bubble, stepped into it and felt the fear, committed myself to doing what had to be done and acted. Then, with a wave of bodily pleasure, the fear bubble burst. All I had to do then was look for the next one.

THE POWER OF ADRENALINE

That night I managed to break my experiences of fear down into episodes that lasted mere minutes – and sometimes just a few seconds. Whereas I'd once treated entire six-month tours as enormous, life-sapping fear bubbles, I'd now reduced them to manageable packets and made my relation-ship with fear completely rational and functional. I realised that while it was surely impossible not to feel fear, it was certainly possible to contain it. It was just a case of working out exactly where the fear was in space and time, then visualising it, before making a conscious choice to step into it and – finally – doing what had to be done.

If it was a surprise how effectively this technique enabled me to manage extreme fear, it was an even bigger surprise to find that it actually made what had sometimes been a horrendous experience almost addictively enjoyable. There was no greater feeling than popping one of those bubbles by going out the other side of it. As soon as I did, I'd experience a surge of adrenaline. I'd use the massive buzz that my adrenaline gave me to propel myself from bubble to bubble. Before long I was running around like a lunatic, looking for the next bubble. Soon, rather than dreading the next moment of danger, I actually began craving it.

People often get fear mixed up with its adrenaline-soaked aftermath. It's important to understand that these are two separate states of mind. It's not uncommon for individuals to confuse one with the other and conclude that they've conquered fear. Instead, adrenaline is a tool. It's a temporary high that powers you on to the next bubble and the next bubble, providing you with the energy and the confidence to keep on going, and giving you the natural high of the reward when you pop each one.

HOW TO HARNESS FEAR

As that tour of duty continued, I began to work out more and more about the fear bubble technique. The final critical lesson I learned was that I didn't have to pop every single bubble that I stepped into. Sometimes I'd enter a bubble, feel all those familiar emotions and sensations blasting up through me, then realise that I wasn't ready for it. It was too much. When operational conditions allowed, I'd step out of the bubble again, take a moment to compose myself and try again. I realised that it was extremely important not to remain in any fear bubble for too long. If I did, those dreadful emotions and sensations would start to drain me. They'd become overwhelming. Then I'd start overthinking my situation and the fear would just grab me and hold me there, frozen to the spot, as all my courage began to weep away. I had to consciously commit to whatever action was necessary to make that bubble pop. If I couldn't do that, I'd step back out of it. Take a moment. Have another go. Too much still? No problem. Step out of it again. Two or three attempts was usually all it took. Ultimately, no bubble ever proved too difficult for me to burst.

TAKING THE BUBBLE HOME

The fear bubble technique not only got me through that tour, it prevented the feeling of dread I'd always experienced between operations from ever coming back. Now that I had my fear compartmentalised and rationalised, and I'd learned to use the natural power of adrenaline to sail me from bubble to bubble, I began to actively look forward to getting out there. My professional life became all about bursting those bubbles. As it did, my performance on the battlefield sky-rocketed. I became a better operator than I'd ever dreamed possible.

And then I returned home. By the time I left the Special Forces, the fear bubble technique had become something that I'd do almost subconsciously. It was just how I handled myself and the various challenges that life threw up. I never considered that it would be transferable to other people until one day I received a message from a sixteen-year-old boy called Lucas who was doing his GCSEs.

After the first series of *SAS: Who Dares Wins* was broadcast, it became normal for me to receive hundreds of messages every week, many of them from young men with various questions about mindset. Often they wanted to join the military or were simply looking for advice on how to cope with certain difficult situations they had coming up. Sadly, I'm only able to respond to a small fraction of these appeals for help. But Lucas sent me a message via social media that I couldn't ignore.

'I just don't want to be on this planet any more,' he wrote.

'What's wrong?' I replied.

'I've got my GCSEs coming up. I'm stressing out. I'm better off not being here. I can't deal with it.'

'Where are you?'

'I'm at home.'

'If you're at home, why are you in that bubble of fear? If you want to get up and have a can of Coke and talk to your parents, you can do that. At this place and time you're in control. You don't need to be in that bubble now. Don't put that pressure on yourself. Even the day of your exams, when you're on your way to school, you don't need to be in that bubble. Even when you open the classroom door and you sit down with the exam paper in front of you, you don't need to be in that bubble. The moment control gets taken away from you and the clock starts ticking, that's when you need to get in the bubble. Attack Question 1 with a bubble. Once you're done with that, come out of it, enjoy the adrenaline, compose yourself, and attack Question 2 with a fresh bubble.'

After I'd properly laid out my own method for dealing with fearful situations, he asked me, 'But why don't I just stay in that bubble for all fifty questions?'

'Because you'll be in it for too long,' I explained. 'What happens if you only know 50 per cent of Question 1? All you're going to do is drag that bubble over to Question 2 and then it's going to negatively affect your performance on that question. And what if you don't know Question 2? The fear will build and build. The negativity will build and build. I guarantee you won't get to Question 10 without your mind starting to frazzle and you losing the plot.'

A couple of weeks later Lucas got back in touch. He had tried my fear bubble technique. And he'd nailed his exam. But it was what he told me afterwards that really got me excited. He said, 'Ant, I loved going from bubble to bubble. It actually made me enjoy the exam.'

I couldn't believe what I was reading. I thought, 'So did I! I used to run around the battlefield looking for the next bubble to get into.' Not only that, but Lucas's performance was dramatically improved by his use of the technique. He reported that his time appreciation was much better and that he actually finished the exam ten minutes early. He came out of his final bubble, looked around and saw that everyone else was still heads down and deep in it.

Hearing all this from Lucas was simply incredible. I never dreamed that this little hack that I'd worked out years previously on a foreign battlefield as a terrified soldier engaging in brutal firefight after brutal firefight could possibly transfer to a GSCE exam hall in Bolton. It was only then that it occurred to me that the technique might have the power to transform other people's lives, just as it had transformed my own.

Eagle-eyed fans of *SAS: Who Dares Wins* might have seen its powerful effects in a famous scene from Series 2. After my experience with Lucas, I thought I'd see if the technique could help the recruits get through some of the tough challenges we throw at them. One capable young contestant called Moses Adeyemi confessed that he was scared of heights and water. Unfortunately for Moses, heights and water were pretty much all we had planned for him in that series. One morning we brought the contestants to a large river into which they'd have to perform a backwards dive from a high platform that we'd erected on top of a shipping container. The moment Moses saw what we had in store for him he began shaking like a leaf.

What the producers of the programme don't have time to show is that, as well as bawling at the contestants and pushing them and punishing them, we also mentor them. When I saw the state that Moses was whipping himself into, I decided to take him off for a couple of minutes and explain the fear bubble technique to him.

'Why are you shaking now?' I asked him. 'You're not in any danger whatsoever. The bubble is on the end of that platform. It's at a place and a time that is not here and is not now. So fucking calm down.'

As I was speaking, Moses was so busy shaking that I thought it was all going completely over his head. But when he walked along the platform a few minutes later, he did so with utter confidence, as if he owned the bloody thing. I watched him get to the very edge, turn around and wobble. That's when I knew he'd grasped it. He was in the bubble. The fear was hitting him.

'You've got this,' I told him.

He tapped his chest three times and muttered something to himself. In that moment I could see that he'd committed. There was no going back now.

And then he dropped. When he was dragged out of the water a couple of minutes later and hauled into the waiting boat, he looked as if he was wired on some sort of illegal drug.

'Easy!' he shouted. 'Fucking easy!'

If I'd asked him to, I'd bet good money that he'd have gladly climbed right back up there and done it all over again.

It's because of my experience with Moses that, whenever we have contestants on *SAS: Who Dares Wins* who have to do something heady like abseil off a cliff, I take the time to talk the really scared ones through the method.

'There's no point standing back here shaking,' I tell them. 'You're wasting your resources. If you keep on thinking like this you won't even get to the edge. Walk up to it, acknowledge the bubble, visualise it, get in it – and then walk back out of it, if you have to. Leave the bubble where it belongs.'

It gets people through, almost every single time. And Moses? That man who was afraid of heights and water, and was lost and trembling in a world of fear filled with heights and water? He ended up being the last man standing, the only one to make it to the very end of that series.

When you make yourself aware of these patterns, you start seeing them everywhere. For example, when people do a bungee jump, they're always terrified before they leap but as soon as the rope takes their weight they're instantly elated. They want to do another jump and then another jump. What's happening is that they're going into the fear bubble, bursting it, and then hitting an adrenaline buzz. That buzz is then pushing them to want to go back into another bubble. When they do go back into that bubble, and do another jump, they're still going to experience a horrible, gut-wrenching dread just before they leap, but this time they know that the moment they pierce it they'll get an instant, massive reward. In this way, bungee jumpers are going through exactly the same process as me on the battlefield, Lucas in the exam hall and Moses in the Ecuadorian rainforest. It becomes enjoyable. It becomes addictive.

THE CORRIDOR

This is when it starts changing your life. When you manage to harness the power of your own fear and go looking for bubbles to pop, amazing things begin to happen. For me, one of these life-changing events took place after I'd left the Special Forces. I'd found some interesting work to do that ended up taking me right across Africa. I spent most of my time on the western side of the continent, in countries such as Senegal, Ivory Coast and Sierra Leone, but every now and then I'd bounce eastwards to Burundi. Often I'd be training government troops in surveillance, counter-surveillance and sniping. One day I found myself working with a team of snipers in Sierra Leone that were about to deploy to Somalia. I was in a troop shelter, unloading their weapons, when my phone rang. It was a withheld number. After hesitating for a moment I decided to answer. On the other end was a posh voice I didn't recognise.

'Are you Ant Middleton?'

'Yes, Ant Middleton speaking.'

'I hear you're the man for the job.'

Who was this joker? After you leave the Special Forces you become used to being approached by all sorts of shady characters offering you all sorts of shady work. You quickly develop an instinct for who's the real deal, and who are the idiots. The first tell is this – the idiots talk as if they're in a bad Guy Ritchie movie. Still, I thought, I might as well hear this one out. To my surprise, he turned out to be an executive from a TV production company. He explained that they were planning on creating a major show in which twenty-five to thirty ordinary men would be put through a condensed version of Special Forces selection. He'd heard I was about the right age bracket and had the right experience. Was I interested in trying out for it, as one of the directing staff?

'I'll call you back,' I said.

My immediate instinct told me that this was a definite no. At that time I was living completely in the shadows. I wasn't on social media, I wasn't in the phone book, I wasn't even on the electoral roll. I was bouncing around Africa, a conti-nent that I love, doing well-paid work, and the only person who knew my whereabouts was my wife Emilie. I was happy with that. Very happy indeed. And, besides, it wasn't seen as the done thing for a Special Forces man to step out of the shadows. What were the lads going to think? How would they take it? When I began to think about the potential ramifications of a television career, a thousand questions suddenly flooded in. I felt my heart begin to pound.

When my mind gets bombarded with questions like this, I always like to take a step back and ask myself the most important question of all. Who am I? I'm someone that loves a challenge. I will challenge absolutely everything. I love opportunity. I will seize every one that comes my way until the end. But my main characteristic is that I love putting myself into situations where I'm forced to sink or swim. I want fear bubbles in my life. I want to be in a world in which I'm having to step into them and pop them in order to move forwards. Everything about this offer scared me. In which case, perhaps I should give it a try.

As it turned out, stepping out of the shadows was indeed a difficult thing to do. After I was approached about the show, I was put under immense pressure from everyone up to Director Special Forces himself not to take part. I was called in for a meeting and told that I would be in breach of my contract if I did it. I didn't believe this was fair.

'You're not paying to put food on my table or a roof over my head, but you still want to dictate the terms of my life,' I said. 'You expect me to live in the shadows even when you're not looking after me any more.'

In that moment I made up my mind. I wasn't going to let them dictate to me.

'I'm doing it. Take me to court.'

I soon discovered that I wasn't the only former operator to tip up as a presenter on the show who'd been through similar meetings and also possessed the fortitude to press on.

The truth is, if I hadn't had my particular relationship with fear, I would never have called that posh guy back. But I did, and it changed everything. Because that's what happens when you live with courage. When my phone rang on that sunny morning in Sierra Leone, it felt as if a door had appeared before me. In front of that door was a fear bubble. After a lot of anxious thinking, I decided to step into that bubble and open that door. And when I went through it, I found myself in a brand new world.

This is all of human life. We live our days in a corridor that's lined with doors. Each one of those doors is frightening to open. This is why, nine times out of ten, we choose to step back from them, leaving them closed. But whenever we muster the courage to step through them, we emerge into a new and better corridor, one that's lined with even more doors that are even scarier to open. Becoming the person we want to be, with the life we've always dreamed of living, is simply a matter of developing the courage to open more doors.

You might not believe that a radical transformation in yourself could be this easy. But it really is. Trust me when I tell you there are two lives you could be living. There's the life you're in right now, at this moment, and there's the better life that's just a step away. Every day that passes without you getting to grips with harnessing your fear means another day that these doors remain shut and you stay limited. I want you to start changing this today. I want you to begin opening these doors. And not only am I going to tell you exactly how to do it, I'm going to show you that it's much easier than you think.

I also want to impress upon you that this should be an urgent mission. You should take it seriously. The sad thing about all these doors you've left closed in your life so far is that you've no idea what lay behind them. You can't imagine who you'd be today if you'd been just a little bit more courageous over the years. But that's enough looking back. I don't want to make you feel regretful or negative. As you'll soon discover, an essential component of the fear bubble technique is the positive mindset. Simply know that your days stuck in that same corridor you've been in for years are now numbered.

WELCOME TO THE FEAR BUBBLE

As you read this book, I want to tell you the story of my journey up Mount Everest. It was during those long days in the spring of 2018, a great many of which were spent quietly putting one foot in front of the other, that much of the thinking you'll find in these pages was done. After that, I want to tell you the story of my coming *down* Everest, which ultimately turned into the most fearful and humbling experience of my life. But most importantly, I want to use my adventures, encounters and conversations on that mountain as a springboard to dive into everything I've learned over the years about how the ability to harness fear and use its power can enable anyone to live without limits.

I'm going to explore how damaging fear can actually be to the individual and everyone around them if it's not contained. Living in fear is corrosive. It creates negativity that spreads throughout a whole life and actually changes the way you perceive reality. Just as it did twenty years ago on Snowdon for the lad just above me who became terrified and suddenly saw the mountain as one huge death trap, fear makes the entire world seem threatening, dangerous and populated by aggressors. This is why living in fear creates a victim mindset – a mindset that's spreading like wildfire in today's society, creating a generation of men and women who seem motivated only to stamp their feet and hope that everyone else will take responsibility for them.

I'll then take a deep look into the three kinds of fear: fear of suffering, fear of failure and fear of conflict. I'll explain how exactly the same fear underlies all of these – the fear that you're not good enough. If you can learn to harness this one – and you can – there will be absolutely no stopping you.

If you've read my previous book, you'll already be familiar with the finer details of my life. After the death of my beloved father, I endured a tough childhood in France with a new stepfather and a mother who forbade any of her children to mourn. I joined the army at seventeen, crashed out at twenty-one, went through a dark period of alcohol abuse, steroid abuse and street violence before finding direction, structure and passion in the Marines, with whom I served a tour of duty in Helmand Province in Afghanistan, and then as an elite operator in the Special Boat Service for four years. When I returned to civvy street in 2011, an altercation with a police officer led me to prison, where I served four months of a fourteen-month sentence for assault. After my release I worked in a variety of jobs that can be very loosely bracketed under the term 'security'. And then I received the call from that posh man from the TV.

But, as I said, if you've read *First Man In* you'll know all this already. The pages you hold in your hands now contain a very different piece of work. That book was my story. This book is my soul.

CHAPTER 3

THE ROAD TO CHOMOLUNGMA

2 APRIL 2017. Qatar Airways Flight 648 from Doha to Tribhuvan International Airport in the Kathmandu Valley. Two hours and twelve minutes until we'd land. A stranger to the left of me, a stranger to the right of me. Perfect. I loved flying alone. The stress of everyday life just melted away, with the white noise of the engines making me feel like I was back in the womb, safe and warm, but with a smiling stewardess bringing me cold cans of beer. I was determined to enjoy the solitude and anonymity while I could. But it wouldn't last long. Because, since I'd cleared this trip with Emilie six months ago, there had been a significant change of plan.

It had happened during a meeting with a TV executive, a couple of weeks after that morning in the kitchen. I'd arrived to discuss the filming of the next two series of *SAS: Who Dares Wins*, which were going to be filmed somewhere in South America.

'We're going to need you guys for a good six weeks,' said the commissioning editor. 'It may even be a couple of months. I guess it depends on how much preparation needs doing and the extent to which you want to get involved in the fine details this time, Ant.'

'I'll want to be involved from the beginning, as always,' I said, reaching for my phone and its calendar app so I could check my dates. 'But I can't do anything April, May time because I'm away.'

'For the whole two months?' he asked.

'Yes, mate,' I said. 'I'm going up Everest.'

He looked at me with an uncomfortable combination of alarm and insult. What was the matter with him?

'That's all right, isn't it?' I said. 'I thought we were think-ing later in the year for *SAS* anyway.'

'Yeah, yeah, sure. It was just, I was wondering – who's covering that, then? Everest?'

It took me a moment to realise what he was thinking.

'What, filming it?' I said. 'Nobody's covering it. It's just a personal thing. I'm not doing a show about it.'

With that, his discomfort melted into glee.

'Well, we should get someone out there with you.'

'Mate, I appreciate the thought, but I don't know about this one,' I said. 'It's kind of a holiday for me. I don't want it to turn into some big production. I just want to keep it small. Me and the mountain.'

'Oh, but we can keep it small,' he said. 'That's no prob-lem. That's easy. We'll strap a fucking GoPro on your hat and send one other dude up there with you.'

'What, up Everest?' I said. 'You can find a cameraman who can keep up, all the way to the summit?'

'I think I can,' he said. 'In fact, I know I can. Ed Wardle. He's been up there like three times or something.'

'To the summit?'

'To the summit. You'd like him. Scottish. He filmed something that was a bit similar to *Mutiny* a few years back. Shackleton's journey. Ernest Shackleton. Is that right? I think that's right. Ernest Shackleton. They went across the Southern Ocean in a little lifeboat using period gear. Proper hardcore. They were living off bowls of, like, cold fat.'

'How far did they go?' I asked.

'Um, can't remember. Something like 800 miles, I think.'

I looked down at my phone and began tapping at the volume buttons distractedly. '800 miles?' I said. 'He wants to try 4,000 miles.'

'Think about it, Ant. Tell me you'll think about it.'

'Yeah, I will,' I said. 'I definitely will.'

I definitely wouldn't. This wasn't what I wanted at all. Part of the attraction of Mount Everest was that there were no rules up on the mountain. I could do what the hell I wanted, take as many risks as I needed to give me that edge I was seeking and generally get into as much trouble as I liked. Having a film crew there, even if it was just one guy, would ruin all that. I wanted to do this thing dangerously. I wasn't going to take the easy route. Other people just didn't understand my level of resilience. They didn't know what I was capable of or what I'd experienced, and I didn't want to be lumbered with well-meaning people, fussing about me, telling me what I could and couldn't do.

In the run-up to *Mutiny* there had been endless pressure from Channel 4 and the production company to do things as sensibly as possible. They'd called all the shots on Health and Safety. I was determined that the trip across the Pacific would be absolutely authentic and fought them all the way on the endless restrictions they kept trying to force upon us. But there was only so much I could do. We ended up making small modifications to the boat and we had nine people compared with the eighteen that went on the original voyage along with Captain Bligh. We were as near as we could be to keeping it real, but I'd have preferred to have kept the things that they removed. The thought of all this nonsense happening to my Everest adventure was not a welcome one.

But then a few weeks passed. And I thought about it. And I kept on going back to the fact that there were five numerals, a comma and a little curly squiggle that made the offer pretty much impossible to refuse. £60,000. The only thing about this trip that had given me reason to doubt its wisdom was the mad cost of it. I was willing to spend the money because I knew that was what it took. But I also had my family to think about. It was a serious amount of cash, and if I could use it for my wife and kids rather than me, and have to sacrifice a little freedom on the mountain to make it happen, then that felt like a trade I simply had to make. If someone else was actually willing to pick up the bill, I felt like I'd have to say yes.

But that compromise soon led to another compromise, one that I was pretty unhappy about. The channel, and the production company, insisted that I book the trip through a different expedition firm. While the track record of Elite Himalayan Adventures was impeccable, they were still quite a young outfit and the terms of the expensive TV insurance they'd have had to take out dictated that we use people experienced with the particular demands of a film crew. That meant a group called Madison Mountaineering, based in Seattle, Washington and founded by Garrett Madison, who bills himself as 'America's premier Everest climber and guide' and has garnered a reputation for taking the 'ultra-wealthy' up to the summit, with luxury trips that cost as much as $120,000. This sounded, to an uncanny extent, like exactly what I didn't want.

Just three days before my flight to Kathmandu I'd come off the final date of my speaking tour. I'd been travelling the country for six weeks, taking my one-man show to theatres from Torquay to Leicester, Cardiff to Manchester, where I was lucky enough to have an audience of 2,500. It had been unbelievably good fun, getting out there and meeting people and hearing their stories, and I'd become so absorbed in the experience that when my departure date from Heathrow came along, it did so suddenly. To say I wasn't mentally prepared for the trip would be an understatement. My head was in a completely different universe, still buzzing from the tour. The idea of going up the highest mountain in the world, in potentially deadly conditions, was one I hadn't even begun getting my head around.

If anything, my physical preparedness was even worse. I'd been eating badly for a month and a half, drinking half a bottle of wine every night and living mainly off chicken wings from the twenty-four-hour room service of the hotels I'd been staying in. I had a lingering memory of Gareth, my tour manager, knocking on my door one night and with a troubled look on his face asking, 'How's the training for Everest going?' I'd picked up my large glass of red wine and toasted him merrily – 'Don't you worry about me.'

On Everest there had been one fatality for every sixteenth person to have successfully climbed it. But I liked those odds. As I lay back on the pillows of my huge hotel bed, in my warm, fluffy hotel dressing-gown, licking Buffalo sauce off my fingertips in preparation for another sip of my nice Shiraz, one in sixteen didn't seem like anything to worry about at all.

And then, on a dull and rainy English spring morning, I found myself packing my luggage into the back of a taxi and going through the ritual of kissing my family goodbye. As I slammed the boot of the cab shut, my two-year-old daughter Priseïs, clinging on to her favourite pink mouse-ear back-pack, suddenly burst into tears as she registered that Daddy was going away somewhere for a long time.

'I know, I know, I know, baby,' I said. But I couldn't calm her.

As my car swung out of the centre of Chelmsford I switched on the little camera that I'd been given to film my journey and pointed it at my face. 'It's never nice saying goodbye. I'm just going to dwell on it for a couple of minutes. Get it out of my system and then get my head in the game.'

I turned the thing off and looked out at the wet trees and the grey motorway. I was close to tears.

But by the time I was pushing up my tray table to prepare for the landing at Kathmandu's Tribhuvan International, that familiar bittersweet sadness was long gone. I was about to alight in a brand new country, one of my most favourite little pleasures. There's not much else that can fill me with such simple childish delight as the sight of an airport sign spelled out in an unfamiliar alphabet.

When I'm in a foreign land it always feels as if the chains have been taken off, especially these days, when it's becoming increasingly hard for me to move about unnoticed. Stepping off the plane in my grey T-shirt and jeans, I could feel the drop in temperature and sense the thin air. A fizz of enthusiasm bubbled up as I walked through the brick building, past adverts for the Everest Bank, and hustled my way impatiently through immigration and then customs. I entered the noisy arrivals hall, weaving my trolley laden with my three bags of kit past endless leather-jacketed men calling, 'Taxi, taxi, do you need a taxi?', and was met by a fixer from Madison Mountaineering, who was holding a little board with my name on.

'Welcome to Kathmandu, Ant!'

Part of the deal for agreeing to have my expedition filmed was that I wasn't going to do it in the luxury style at which Madison, in particular, excelled. Any normal commercial expedition up Everest involves a large team of people led by Western guides and supported by teams of local Sherpas, who all work with between ten and twenty clients at any one time. As you'd expect, these companies can and do ply their trade with safety as a top priority. One of the biggest dangers on Everest concerns the many problems that come as a result of the lack of available oxygen. This is not just an issue in the death zone. People can fall sick, become confused and make perilously bad decisions even down at Base Camp, which sits at over 5,000 metres above sea level, where there's 50 per cent less oxygen in the air than in the lowlands.

To try to combat this, Westerners are taken up the hill slowly. When you're ascending from sea level to nearly the cruising altitude of a jumbo jet, you need to allow your body to become used to the conditions as gradually as possible. This is why climbers use a system of 'rotations' to acclimatise. Having first done the long trek to Base Camp, where they can stay for two weeks or more, the rotations start with the ascent from there to Camp I, where they stay for two nights. Then it's a couple of nights in Camp II and then back down to Base Camp again. The second rotation is the same, with the addition of Camp III. It's pretty standard to complete a third rotation. And then, finally, you get to do the summit rotation.

That sounded like a lot of hassle to me. I didn't think I could be bothered to complete three rotations only to have to start all over again from Base Camp to get to the top. I decided I'd see how I felt when I got on the mountain, but I honestly didn't feel the need to be as careful as all the other Westerners. I wasn't there for my health and safety.

And there were also some other ways in which I intended to do my climb differently to most. I made it clear to Madison Mountaineering that, as far as possible, I'd be my own boss. While they would take care of all the general organisation, and I'd stay in their camps and make use of their supplies of food, drink and oxygen, I wasn't going to be chucked in with all their wealthy clients. I didn't want to be part of any tour group. I also refused the help of their Western guides. My expedition was just going to be me, a Sherpa, Ed to film us and another Sherpa for him. And unlike all the other fresh-faced visitors, I wasn't going to rely on Sherpas to lug my stuff up the hill. Westerners are some-times guilty of viewing the locals as little more than mules – I wasn't going to be one of them, and I would carry my own kit.

'Your Sherpa's outside waiting to meet you,' said Madison's American fixer, trying to take my trolley off me so she could push it. 'His name is Dawa Lama. And your cameraman Ed's here too.'

'Thank you,' I said, politely but insistently pulling my trolley back.

As soon as I left the airport building I clocked Ed. He was walking towards me with his large camera held at chest height and his headset on. I'd heard that this tall Scottish hard-man was an alpha, and he certainly appeared to be a very capable individual. He was six foot five, lightly grizzled and looked to be in his forties. He was fit and lean in his untucked shirt, black trousers and hiking boots. I realised it was important that our relationship struck the right balance from the outset. I knew, from sore experience, that having two alphas working closely together could be difficult, and it usually requires some precise handling. A couple of days earlier he'd called me so we could make our final arrangements to meet and begin the process of getting to know each other. When I answered the phone, he said, 'I'm on Ben Nevis.' Obviously it was necessary that he called, but why do it from the highest mountain in Britain unless you're making a point? He seemed like a decent and smart guy when we chatted, but that phone call had put me on slight alert. I thought, 'Let's see how this pans out.'

Although I was happy to meet Ed in the flesh, as soon as I saw his camera pointing at me I felt my heart sink. It wasn't the fact of the camera itself, it was all the attention that being filmed naturally draws towards you. You become instantly highlighted. Lines of blue-uniformed policemen stared at us, as did all the porters, drivers and tourists who were milling about the busy airport parkway. I could see them squinting at me thinking, 'Who in the hell's that?' It was a sudden reminder of the compromise I'd made in allowing this thing to be filmed. If I'd arrived alone, as planned, I'd have been feeling utterly free and joyful right about now.

As I approached the smiling Scotsman, I had to give myself a little pep talk: 'This is my thing. He's following me up a mountain. I'm not going to let him take my trip over and turn it into a "show".' I made a promise to myself. My attitude towards Ed was always going to be, 'Follow me. If you get your footage, you get it. If you don't, you don't.'

'How you doing, mate?' I said, shaking his hand. 'You good?'

'Yes, mate,' he said. He fixed me with a slightly quizzical look. 'Do you realise what you've got yourself into?'

That got my guard up. In his own subtle way it seemed that Ed was instantly questioning my ability. The skill set involved in being a member of the Special Forces is a lot different to what's needed by an elite mountaineer, and he knew it. Not only that, but since our chat on the phone the other day he knew I'd only ever been as high as 6,100 metres above sea level. That's pretty high, but it's not Everest. The whole situation threatened to put me on the back foot immediately. I could tell that Ed was extremely sure of himself and didn't take any shit. He'd be an easy guy to get on with if he respected you, but he didn't suffer fools. Quiet worries crowded in on me: 'Am I going to have to live up to his standards? Am I going to have to follow him up to the summit?'

Although he was probably acting subconsciously, I couldn't ignore the fact that he was trying to assert himself as the leader from the start. While I knew it wasn't a personal thing – it's just what alphas do – I also knew I had to turn it around. And quickly. It would have been the easiest thing in the world to have stepped back and let him take the reins. It would even have made logical sense, given that he was by far the more experienced mountaineer. But I wasn't going to allow Ed to make the decisions. I couldn't ever have a situation in which he was telling me, 'Well, Ant, there's a bit of wind today so we best go tomorrow.' A bit of wind? Good. All the more reason to go now. This trip was mine and I was doing it for my own reasons. They'd jumped on my bandwagon, not the other way round.

And then, out from behind Ed, as if by magic, appeared the man who would be my Sherpa. Dawa Lama had been picked especially for me by Madison and I was a bit shocked when I saw him. I'm only small myself, but Dawa was positively tiny. Not only was he five foot nothing in height, he had a bit of weight on him. I'd imagined someone a bit more trim and a lot taller. Was this really the man who'd be leading me up the world's most deadly mountain? But he had to be capable, I told myself. He wouldn't have been selected if he wasn't. The only way we were going to find out what he was made of was by getting him up on that hill.

Dawa was holding a garland of marigold flowers and I bent down so he could put it around my neck. I could instantly tell that getting on with him wasn't going to be a problem. He radiated a kind of natural, easy-going warmth.

'Welcome to Nepal,' he said, shaking my hand.

I pulled him up into a bear hug. As I did, the sky above us blasted into a fantastic rip of thunder.

'That's what I love to hear, mate. That gets me excited,' I said. 'Are you ready, Dawa?'

'Yeah,' he said.

'Are you sure, brother?'

'Yeah.'

This was my opportunity to signal to Ed that it was me who'd be calling the shots.

'Are you ready, Ed?'

'I'm ready.'

'Are you sure?'

He didn't reply. He just laughed. That, I figured, was him signalling back.

As we walked towards our transport, I said to him, half-joking, 'I hope you're going to keep up with me. Anywhere I go, just make sure you capture it.'

'Oh, I will,' he said. 'You know it can be pretty hard going up there. Are you sure you've done enough preparation?'

There it was again.

'Don't worry about me, mate,' I said. But in the depths of my mind I had a sudden, panicked flash of a bowl of chicken wings glistening with Buffalo sauce.

The transport to the hotel turned out to be a tiny white banger with holes in the floor and just enough room for the three of us. We rattled off into the thick of the city, a grinding metropolis of traffic, noise, brightly painted concrete apartments, temple roofs glimpsed down tangled alleyways, fluttering prayer flags and potholed roads, all set in a haze of filthy, smoggy air. Despite my background concerns about Ed, I found myself high on the spirit of adventure, which is the greatest buzz I know. The giddy mood had become infectious and we were all grinning widely. I decided to use it to help us bond as a team as quickly as we could. Right now that meant indicating to Dawa that he wasn't going to be treated as an employee but as one of us. Even though I was determined that I would make all the key decisions, it was Dawa who'd be in charge of the route we'd be taking. His role in my expedition couldn't be more crucial.

'How many times have you summited?' I asked him.

'I've summited six times on the top, and eleven times expeditions,' he said. 'First time was when I was nineteen. With my father.'

'Was he a Sherpa too?'

'Yes,' he said. 'And he is still working on the mountain today.'

I looked down at the flowers he'd strung around my neck. 'What are these for?'

'For good luck.'

'Good luck? Listen,' I said, patting him on the shoulder. 'That's for the unprepared.' I thought for a moment. Those chicken wings again. 'But hey. We'll see. We might need it.'

'Tonight you and Ed are coming to eat at my house,' he said proudly. 'It's all arranged. I have booked a car for 7 p.m. It will pick you up at the Yak and Yeti Hotel where you're staying. My wife is cooking a welcome meal that is special.'

'That would be an honour,' I said. 'Thank you, Dawa.'

Not only would it be an honour; it would also provide the perfect opportunity to strengthen our relationship. He didn't yet know it, but it wasn't only the route up to the summit that Dawa would be finding. He'd also be essential in getting me to that edge of fear I was going to be secretly hunting. One of the reasons I didn't want a Western guide was because, as you'd expect, they tend to be ultra-cautious. They wouldn't want the negative publicity of having any of their clients lose a nose, a couple of toes – or their life. But a Sherpa, I expected, would be willing to push that little bit harder. If I said to a Western guide, 'Let's go up through that storm,' they'd most likely refuse and maybe even turn us around. You'd hope a Sherpa would be more game. After all, they live close by the mountain. It wasn't 'Mount Everest' to them, it was 'Chomolungma', a living god. They'd known that mysterious lump of ice and rock, and its shifting, deadly moods, for thousands of years. It was in their blood.

Contrary to what many people assume, 'Sherpa' isn't a job title but the name of an ethnic group of people who live in this region and out towards Bhutan, India and Tibet. There are over 110,000 Sherpas in Nepal, a country with a population of more than 20 million, and the heartland of their people is the region known as the Khumbu, a series of deep, rocky valleys that lie at the base of Everest's southern slopes.

The Sherpa have always been an essential component of Everest expeditions, in part on account of their local knowledge, in part because of various genetic adaptations that enable them to operate at an almost miraculous capacity at high altitudes. In ordinary humans, who have evolved to live mainly in the world's lowlands, climbing 2,500 metres or higher above sea-level without acclimatisation has the potential to trigger mountain sickness, as the body begins to suffer from the lack of available oxygen in the air. Among the condition's milder symptoms are headaches, ringing in the ears, nausea, loss of appetite, shortness of breath, insomnia and depression. At its worst, it can kill you.

Physiological reactions arising from a lack of oxygen have taken the lives of a great many highly capable individuals on Everest. If the body is deprived of oxygen for too long, the brain will swell and the lungs will flood, as the liquid that usually lines the blood vessels leaks into them and accumulates in deadly pools, causing high-altitude cerebral oedema (HACE) in one case and high-altitude pulmonary oedema (HAPE) in the other. At best, the need to breathe such thin and cold air so rapidly means that most climbers get some form of high-altitude cough as a result of their lungs drying out. It's not the kind of cough a couple of Halls Soothers can tackle, either. It can get so bad that it breaks your ribs.

But Sherpas are far less susceptible to such problems, thanks to some amazing tweaks that have been made to their bodies by the forces of evolution. Eight thousand years of mountain life have given them a host of biological super-powers. Their lungs have greater capacity than ours, mean-ing that they can both inhale air more rapidly and draw in more oxygen with each breath. Adaptations to the engineer-ing of their blood system also make them more efficient at high altitudes. When there's not enough oxygen in the air, the body has to kick in to an emergency state, part of which involves pumping more red blood cells into your system. This is because it's the red blood cells that carry oxygen to your brain, and your muscles now find themselves in desper-ate need of it. But producing more red blood cells has the side-effect of thickening your blood, which makes it harder to pump.

All this extra work puts your body under huge stress. Soon the blood can become so thick that your blood vessels begin to clog up. When Sherpas reach high altitudes, however, their bodies don't produce as many of these red blood cells as those of lowlanders, which means their blood doesn't run so thick. Not only that; they have much higher levels of a chemical called nitric oxide in their blood, which opens up the blood vessels and keeps everything flowing properly. If all that wasn't enough, Sherpa bodies are also more efficient at generating energy. It's for these reasons, and more, that some scientists have gone so far as to call them 'superhuman'.

This is not to say that it's in any way easy for a Sherpa to reach the summit of Everest. It's still a remarkable feat and the risks remain plentiful. No amount of evolution can prevent a man falling into a crevasse, being crushed by an avalanche or being frozen to death in sub-zero gale-force winds. Sherpas account for roughly 40 per cent of all the climbers who have died on the slopes of Chomolungma. That serial killer of a mountain doesn't discriminate. When it wants bodies, it takes them.

That evening, at bang on 7 p.m., Ed and I climbed into the taxi that Dawa had ordered to pick us up from the Yak and Yeti Hotel. I was glad to leave. It was a nice enough place but it was teeming with mountaineers and trekkers, and I was keen to get away from all those rosy-cheeked Western faces.

We soon arrived at Dawa's place, and he opened a wooden door that led into a warm central room that had several other doors leading off it. On the opposite side was the kitchen, and the sound of crackling pans and smells of cooking wafted in from it on a welcoming cloud. Dawa's wife came in when she heard us enter, her hands wet from the cooking, her face flushed and beaming.

'Namaste,' she said, bowing slightly and pressing her palms together as if in prayer.

This traditional greeting means 'I salute the God within you.' That was my kind of greeting. We namaste'd back and lowered our necks to receive more garlands of flowers from our pretty host, and then their children started streaming out of one of the doors. 'Namaste! Namaste!' they chanted, their little hands in steeples, before vanishing as quickly as they'd appeared.

With all this bowing and ceremony, it was clear that having Ed and me coming into Dawa's home to eat was a serious occasion for them. This wasn't just popping round your mate's place for a couple of Domino's. Dawa invited us to sit at the low table in the centre of the room and we arranged ourselves cross-legged around it. His wife went back into the kitchen and brought us cups of warm and spiced milky tea, a little like chai. As we sipped, I noticed that photos of his family were arranged in frames all over the walls.

'Is that your father?' I asked, pointing to one large picture near the fireplace.

'He's one of the oldest Sherpa still working the mountain,' he told me. 'He's also a lama.'

This was truly impressive. In Nepal, the Sherpas who assist expeditions to the very summit of Everest receive as much honour and respect as those who join the famous Gurkhas. But the climbers have something that the military operators lack: money. In a country in which the average annual salary is around $700, Everest's Sherpas can take home $5,000 over the course of a two-month season. That's the equivalent of someone in the UK bringing in a couple of hundred grand. Additionally, it's seen as the done thing to tip your Sherpa $1,000 if he gets you right to the top. These men can end up extremely wealthy, at least by local standards, and most of the accommodation that tourists stay in along the route to Base Camp is owned by them.

Quite aside from the money, many of the local guides are no less obsessed with mountaineering than the majority of their clients. They're addicted to the mountain. There's huge competition among the young men of the Khumbu to become one of the four hundred or so guys who are hired every year by Western expedition firms. So to hear that Dawa's father was not only one of the most senior Sherpas on the mountain but also a lama – a Buddhist teacher and priest – was an indication that he was an extremely important individual.

As we chatted, Dawa's wife started laying out delicious-looking food on the table in front of us. There were bowls of rice, flatbreads and what turned out to be a huge serving of thukpa, a dense noodle soup filled with extra-wide noodles, broth, vegetables and big lumps of chicken. Dawa motioned for us to start digging in, but I noticed that his wife had disappeared back into the kitchen.

'I'm not eating until she sits down,' I said.

'OK,' he laughed.

'Come on out here!' I shouted after her.

She appeared back in the doorway and I shuffled across to give her space to sit beside me.

'And the children?' I said. 'Where are they? Get them in here!'

With that, Dawa's smile dropped just slightly.

'The children will eat after.'

Whenever I'm travelling I always want to respect the culture of the country I'm in. For me, there's no better way to do that than by actually living it, socialising with the locals, drinking the same beer, eating the same food, learning about the rules of the land from the people you meet. I never set out to offend anyone, but, at the same time, I'll always be me. When you're in a new place, you don't want to curl up in a ball and think, 'Oh, what if I say the wrong thing?' because that stops you from connecting on a human level. It creates tension. I'd rather say something that's not quite right, like inviting the kids to eat with us, and then have a laugh about it, than not say anything at all.

Living in a fearful mindset cripples all parts of your life, and, in my experience, the fear of giving offence creates more problems than it solves. Ultimately what you're scared of is that your hosts won't like you because you've, say, thrown a chewing-gum wrapper on the fire. But most people are reasonable. They will understand your weird foreign ways and will happily shrug them off. What's much more likely is for them not to like you because you're tense and patronising and come across as if you're not embracing them on that human level. It was crucially important for me and my mission that Dawa gained the impression that I was going to be easy to get along with. This wasn't going to happen if I was anxious about every little thing I said and did.

The food was even more delicious than it looked, and I caught Ed's eye as we tucked in. He was clearly enjoying the thukpa as much as I was.

'Do you worry about Dawa when he's not here?' I asked his wife.

'No, it would make me put more pressure on him. I don't want to do that,' she said. 'Dawa loves his job and provides for us all. Everything you see here is because he loves what he's doing. He's lost some good friends on the mountain, but it was their time. It is not yet Dawa's time.'

I turned to Dawa. 'Is that right? You've lost some friends? Tell me.'

'Three years ago,' he said. 'The avalanche.'

The 2014 avalanche was one of the deadliest disasters to ever take place on Everest. It struck on a particularly fearsome part of the normal route up the mountain from the Nepalese side known as the Khumbu Icefall. The icefall is, as it sounds, a steep and enormous channel of ice that climbers have no choice but to climb through. It forms the bottom end of the glacier that spills out of a glacial cirque called the Western Cwm, above which the summit of Everest soars high up to the north. Starting not far from Base Camp at around 5,500 metres above sea level, it's made up of enormous blocks of ice, called seracs, that are in a state of constant if mostly imperceptible motion as they descend the mountain under the force of gravity. It's a landscape straight out of some horror-fantasy novel. It's alive. It's moving. And it wants to eat you.

Because the icefall moves so much – the seracs collapsing and new crevasses opening up – a completely new route has to be found through it at the start of every climbing season. A system has been agreed in which the Sherpas associated with a different nominated expedition company take responsibility for doing so every year. It involves laying aluminium ladders across its yawning crevasses and fixing ropes into place up sheer ice cliffs over which streams of paying clients will eventually be led.

On 18 April, it turned out, several of Dawa's friends were part of the route-fixing team. They were working deep in a section of the icefall known as the 'Popcorn Field', because it comprises hundreds of towering seracs that, when seen from above, resemble a great bowl of the stuff. It was around a quarter to seven in the morning and they were busily fixing ropes when a massive chunk of ice – about the size of an office block, roughly thirty-five metres thick and weighing over fourteen million kilos – came loose from high on the mountain's western shoulder. It smashed directly into the icefall. Twenty-five men were buried. Sixteen died. Some of their bodies are still up there.

'But your friends dying doesn't stop you wanting to climb?' I said. 'It doesn't give you too much fear?'

'To our people Chomolungma is a sacred mountain, and it either grants you passage or it does not.'

'But how do you know if it's granted you passage?'

'Before we climb, we have a ceremony. A puja. We ask Chomolungma permission to climb.'

'Will I get to take part in a puja?'

'Of course,' he said. 'You must. Only then will we climb.'

In that moment, Dawa's love for what he did was palpable. Not only was I impressed by his passion; I also quite understood his outlook. Although it had a thick religious overlay, I could see it for what it actually was – a positive mindset. Yes, he had every reason to feel overwhelming fear on that mountain, but he'd told himself a story that enabled him to handle the fear. This was the method that his Buddhist culture had evolved, over many thousands of years, to enable people like him to step into that fear bubble and commit to the task ahead. Despite the enormous differences in our backgrounds and spiritual beliefs, I realised we were strikingly similar people. I understood him. This was the connection that I'd been seeking.

Before we left, I wanted to glean as much knowledge as I could on how to tackle the mountain as smartly as possible.

'How do we handle the altitude rises?' I asked him. 'What's the maximum we should be doing in a day?'

'Five hundred, six hundred metres a day is good,' he said. 'No more than a thousand. The best advice is to take it slow, slow, slow.'

'But I don't want to be hanging around too long in the camps waiting for my body to adjust. I just want to crack into it. Get it done.'

'Well, the best trick is to make sure your body's acclimatising as you're walking,' he said. 'Other people, they try to get from one camp to another as quickly as possible, and then they're stopping there to let their body acclimatise. But if you climb too fast, you'll end up lying about in the camp for much longer. We should stay moving up on the mountain, above Base Camp, as long as we can.'

With Dawa's sound advice ringing in our ears, Ed and I left his house feeling good. It felt as if, in my own small way, I was beginning to get into the Sherpa mindset. The ultimate goal would be to become a Sherpa as much as is humanly possible – to eat like a Sherpa, sleep like a Sherpa, think like a Sherpa. I was ready to soak up not just the raw facts about the mountain that Dawa knew, but everything he was.

* * *

THAT ENCHANTING SHERPA spell that had been weaved about us didn't last long. The next evening, Ed and I met for dinner in the bar of the Yak and Yeti Hotel. As we waited for our pepperoni pizza two men in their early forties, wearing box-fresh North Face fleeces and with matching Oakley mirrored shades propped on their foreheads, strode up to our table. They had huge grins on their faces. What did these jokers want?

'Well, well, well,' said one, in a West Coast American accent. 'Mr Edward Wardle! As I live and breathe.'

It quickly became apparent that they knew Ed from previous climbs. After he'd made the introductions, the three of them fell automatically into that typical dick-swinging chatter. *What expedition are you with? I've done this, I've done that. I've made it to the surface of the sun and back in a little pair of pink swimming trunks* ... I sipped my beer quietly, listening to it all.

'So, Ant, have you summited?' said one of them.

'No, mate,' I said.

And, with that, I completely vanished from their vision. It was incredible. I had simply ceased to exist for them. And I had no comeback at all. They continued talking around me, making it clear that I'd been deemed unworthy to enter their conversation. I sat there fuming, thinking, 'You summit wankers.' I found myself staring at the ashtray on the table. It looked heavy. *You could do some damage with that.*

'Oooh, part of the Summit Club are you?' I said to Ed, once they'd gone.

He laughed. 'Yeah, sorry about that, Ant,' he said. 'I know. They're good guys, they're just high on that start-of-the-season buzz, that's all.'

I ate my dinner and left for my room as soon as I could. I was beginning to feel like I was on a package holiday. I couldn't wait to get out of there and into the Himalayan wilds.

I woke early the next morning, prepared my kit, and we took off in a tiny blue and white twelve-seater plane for the short flight from Kathmandu to the hill town of Lukla. After we'd risen out of the city, we quickly found ourselves flying into a land of black and white, a vast realm of the sky constructed purely of cloud, snow and ice, and dark, jagged peaks. Soon our aircraft banked, then abruptly dived, and we began our descent into Tenzing–Hillary Airport. This was going to be fun. Lukla's airport is the world's most dangerous, mostly on account of its airstrip, which, at just 500 metres, is also the world's shortest. The last serious crash here, in October 2008, killed all eighteen passengers. Somehow the pilot survived.

We rattled down towards it at speed. Looking out of my window, I could see what looked to be a shanty town laid out on the ground beneath me. Suddenly, the scene shook into a blur as the plane hit the ground and the pilot rammed on the brakes. It was an impressive bit of airmanship – the airstrip looked more like a dead-end road in a residential neighbourhood than a place to land a plane.

Sitting at the entrance to a deep, rocky valley at an altitude of 2,805 metres, Lukla translates as 'the place of many goats and sheep'. These days it's a place of lodges, restaurants and shops selling T-shirts that say, 'My boyfriend went up Everest and all I got was this lousy T-shirt'. As well as all the tourists, the place was filled with porters hanging around and waiting to be employed. These men are picked by Sherpas, who know them all by sight and select their favourites – 'You, you, you …' It's these guys who work the trekking trail, going back and forth between Lukla and Base Camp but no further, carrying their clients' heavy bags. One step beneath the porters are the yak boys, who load up their massive, obedient animals with the heaviest equipment and guide them along the path.

As we left Lukla and started our ten-day trek to Base Camp along the Namche Trail, I felt newly excited. We headed north, out of the busy hill town, through an ancient-looking white archway that was topped with an ornate pinnacle and lined with golden prayer wheels. In my day sack I had warm kit, gloves, vests, socks, water, enough food to sustain me for twenty-four to thirty-six hours, a GPS, spare batteries and a handheld camera. I was happy and I was prepared. Life was good.

It didn't take long, however, before the effects of the altitude started to make themselves known. I developed a dull headache and felt mildly nauseous, and soon realised that I was becoming uncharacteristically irritable. It didn't help that the trail was much busier than I'd anticipated. We found ourselves having to pick our way past endless flocks of trekkers, with their spiked poles and packed lunches. That morning we stopped at a waypoint showing that more than 50,000 trekkers had passed through it during the previous year, and that didn't include anyone from any of the Everest expeditions.

'How does that make you feel?' asked Ed.

'Not special,' I replied.

But the scenery began making up for it. On either side of the rocky trail, forests of trees rose precipitously up the foothills. We passed fields and meadows, then picked our way up gorges, crossing impossibly high and narrow suspension bridges that spanned wide valleys whose winding rivers were so far down that they could be glimpsed but not heard. Tattered prayer flags in red, yellow and blue flapped and twisted in the Himalayan air while musky-smelling yaks, laden with bags, trudged stoically along, their clanging bells making a soft and rhythmic accompaniment to the monotony of one-foot-in-front-of-the-other.

Every so often we'd pass through small, ragged trail towns – Choplung, Phakding, Toktok – their simple buildings covered with painted corrugated tin roofs, their dusty lanes marked with prayer wheels and painted stones. The lamas of the village would bless us as we passed, beating drums and throwing rice. It was in these towns that we'd sleep, in tea huts that were like one-star hotels. They had outdoor toilets, and every guest was issued with a thin mattress and a wooden bed on which to unroll their sleeping bag before stretching out. At the end of every day, after smashing out eight to ten hours of solid hiking, I wanted to enjoy the sense of achievement and adventure I felt that I'd earned. But I kept on finding myself sitting across from Roger and Beryl from Royal Tunbridge Wells, sipping their Earl Grey from their little fucking flasks and insistently trying to make conversation with me about their grandkids' GCSEs.

'I'm fed up with the tourists,' I quietly confessed to Dawa the following morning over a breakfast of boiled eggs and black coffee. 'How long is it going to be like this? All the way to Base Camp?'

Dawa nodded thoughtfully.

I looked up, squinting into the sun, towards a distant mountain pinnacle.

'I wanted to get that sense of isolation and adventure,' I said. 'I wanted to learn about Sherpa culture from the inside. But I feel like I'm in some sort of theme park. Does that make sense?'

I was glad I spoke up because it gave Dawa an idea.

'Well, if you like we can go on a quieter route. It is off the trail. We can head up to Khumjung. This is a Sherpa village. It is where we live off season.'

'Is Khumjung far?' asked Ed.

'It will take us out of our way for maybe two days,' he said.

I didn't need to give it a second thought. 'Let's do it.'

Khumjung was exactly what I needed – a large village at an altitude of 3,780 metres, huddled in a mountain basin, and overlooked by the peaks of Thamserku and Ama Dablam. It was a place of white dry-stone walls and weather-worn, green-roofed buildings, with a huge football pitch at its edge. It was all local people, their children playing in the streets and watching us with bored curiosity from doors and windows.

Dawa led me to the place where we'd be sleeping, a hut owned by a Sherpa friend of his called Surki. We walked into a small room. A large PVC poster of a Western-style house with a shiny black SUV on the drive was stuck to one wall, and strings of plastic flowers hung in the corners. I shook the hand of a little girl who gazed up at me with a look of vague confusion from the edge of a bed.

'Namaste!' I said.

This was going to be fun.

Later that afternoon we sat down with Surki. He was an old fella, perhaps in his early sixties, wearing big spectacles, a woolly Everest hat and a brand new blue puffa.

'We're planning on going to the summit,' I told him.

'Well, be careful,' he said.

'We will. What's it like, Everest?'

His face transformed itself into a huge, joyful smile.

'Delicious,' he said. 'One hundred per cent delicious.'

When I told Surki about my plan to get my head into the real Everest by living and thinking like a Sherpa, he started excitedly pointing at a red and black bowl that was heaped with what looked like sawdust.

'Tsampa,' he said, passing to me. I wasn't sure, but I think he wanted me to eat it.

'This is better than a porridge or a toast,' explained Dawa.

'It's like Sherpa oxygen?' I volunteered.

'More than oxygen!' cried Surki delightedly.

He showed us how to prepare it, by mixing it into a glass of cold water. I watched him take a huge gulp of the now beige liquid, clumps of powder still clinging to the rim of his glass. I spooned a healthy dose of it into my own cup and took a tentative sip. It felt kind of greasy, with congealed lumps floating about in it, and tasted exactly as nice as it looked. Ed pointed the camera at me, perhaps hoping for that classic TV moment in which I pronounced the local fare absolutely delicious.

'That,' I said, running my tongue along my teeth, which were coated in a film of slimy powder, 'is not nice.'

'One hundred per cent oxygen!' laughed Surki.

'If it's good enough for the Sherpas,' I said, 'it's good enough for me.'

I gave the glass a final rapid stir and downed the lot.

I slept that night in all my clothes on a cold and comfort-less bench, covered only by a thin sheet. It felt great.

BY SEVEN O'CLOCK the next morning, Dawa, Ed and I left Khumjung on a wide, rock-strewn track. After a hard morn-ing's hike, we rounded the corner into another Sherpa village. The path ran downwards, past one of the large Buddhist shrines that had by now become a familiar sight. The cloud cover had begun to clear, with clumps of mist still stubbornly clinging to the rocky valley walls on either side of us. The altitude was affecting me more and more. There was a dull ache, like a clenched fist, in the centre of my skull and my breathing was becoming noticeably more laboured. My appetite was also starting to suffer – although, to be fair, that might have been the after-effects of that tsampa from the night before.

But these first pangs of altitude sickness were no match for the force of my mood. I finally felt some of the isolation I'd been craving. Added to that, we were enjoying what is often the best part of any adventure, right at the start when you know you've still got everything to come. Because we weren't yet up on the mountain, my relationship with Ed hadn't so far been properly tested, but he was proving to be excellent company, and seemed happy to take a step back and let me have my head.

As we turned into the village and onto a high plateau, a beautiful sight presented itself in the far distance. Whereas the mountains to either side of us were the colour of dark khaki, these impossible-looking peaks at the end of the valley were covered in a layer of snow that, under the newly bright sky, glowed with a heavenly brightness.

'Wow, look at that view,' I said.

'Everest,' said Dawa.

I couldn't believe it. What did he just say? I stopped in my tracks.

'Where's Everest?'

He pointed straight ahead of us.

'No,' I said. 'Really? You're joking me?'

'No.'

'What, there?' I pointed at a pyramid of dark rock that rose imperiously above the snowy slopes.

'Yes.'

'You're joking me, Dawa. Are you serious?'

'Yes,' he said, gripping into my shoulder. 'Everest.'

It was almost overwhelming. I wasn't sure if it was the altitude, but I experienced a moment of intense disorientation. The mountain suddenly seemed so close to us. I'd imagined that we were a million miles away but it was right there in front of me, almost as if I could grab it out of the sky. But then, in an instant, my perspective shifted. Now it appeared a universe away, an unbelievably arduous challenge. How the hell were we going to get up *that*?

And suddenly I realised I was in the presence of the prey I'd been secretly stalking since we'd landed in the Khumbu. I could feel it in my heart and in my gut.

There it was.

The fear.

CHAPTER 4

THE MAGIC SHRINKING POTION

I WILL NEVER forget that moment I first laid eyes on Mount Everest. Not only was it more beautiful and more staggering than I ever imagined it would be; it also instantly transported me back twenty years. As I stood there next to Dawa in a state of awe, not quite sure if I believed what he was telling me, I had that moment of disorientation that always occurs when sudden fear has its devious way with my mindset. When I looked upon the scene with excitement, the mountain seemed so close that I could kiss it. But when the dread kicked in, it zoomed away, too far for me to ever catch up, and began looming over the landscape like some threatening beast.

Whenever anything of this sort happens, I always remember being that scared youngster up on Snowdon climbing a narrow track of scree and ice. I can feel, once again, the tense feeling of sickness in my gut as I realised that if I took just a couple of steps to my right I'd be dead. When you let fear overwhelm you like that, it's as if the whole world rearranges itself in opposition to you. It feels like you're utterly surrounded by traps and enemies, as though the purpose of the universe itself is to take you down. It feels personal.

It was because of this mindset of fear that the lad in front of me decided he couldn't go any further. When he pressed his weight down on a loose rock and watched it separate from the mountainside and fly away into the abyss – a chance incident that didn't physically harm him in any way – it destroyed him mentally. Snowdon became a hostile being to him. It was alive. It was a monster. It wanted to kill him. I felt it too. As I pressed myself into the loose track, to let him and his shaking limbs spider back down past me, I was on the brink of going with him. 'He could have died,' I thought. 'And I could bloody die too.' Snowdon had transformed into one giant fear bubble.

But then something happened. A shout came from below me. 'What you doing, Midsy? Come on!' That shout forced me to make a decision, one way or the other. I had to commit. As soon as I did, the entire world changed. That mountain didn't want to kill me any more. It wanted to help me.

What I've come to realise is that there are two ways of experiencing reality. Neither of them is entirely accurate, but all of us live our days in one of these skewed versions of reality or the other. Some of us are positive thinkers. We tend to see the world as a place filled with challenges and charge at it, excited about the possibilities that every new day brings. We love being in that corridor of life, busting through door after door and changing and growing as we step into new corridor after new corridor. We fall down and fail as much as anyone else. But when we do, we don't take it personally. We pick ourselves up, chalk it up to experience and crack on.

The other people are the negative thinkers. They see the world as full of danger, and are daunted by the threats and hurdles that every new day brings. They're stuck in the same corridor, day after day, year after year, never opening any of the doors that are presented to them. Whenever they fall down and fail, they take it personally. Things went wrong because this person is out to get them, or that person is a bully or a bigot or a bitch or a bastard, or because the system is unfair and fixed against them, or because of something bad that happened to them twenty, thirty, forty years ago. Sadly this seems to be a much more common way of viewing reality. And it's spreading. More and more people these days are allowing themselves to be taken over by this victim mindset. It's my belief that the cause of this mindset is fear.

A VICTIM IN THE FAMILY

Why am I convinced that this negative, victim mindset is rooted in fear? Because I've witnessed the entire process happening inside my childhood home. It all began with the strange and sudden death of my father, Peter Aaron, an event that obviously left me and all three of my brothers devastated.

Even today I treasure memories of the family on holiday in Australia, watching him mucking about in a swimming pool on a perfect sunny day, for some reason with two white kittens in his hands. Dad, who worked as a software engineer for IBM, was a gentle and kind man addicted to chocolate digestive biscuits. He taught me to ride my bike. He could hardly have been more different from my stepfather, Dean, a severe younger man who suddenly appeared on the scene as our 'new dad', literally the day after our real dad's death.

As the third-oldest child, I'd never had the opportunity to get to know Dad as well as my two older brothers did. I was only five when he died, while Michael was seven and Daniel was eight. My little brother Peter was just three and can't really remember him to this day. Being the eldest, it seemed to hit Daniel the hardest of all. As I've already mentioned, one of the odd and deeply unpleasant facts about Dad's death was that my mum and Dean wouldn't allow us to mourn him. Immediately after that horrible day when his body was removed from the house, all our pictures of him were removed and we were strictly forbidden from mention-ing his name. We weren't even allowed to go to his funeral. The only photo I ever saw of Dad was at my grandfather's house. It was of the two men smiling together and was kept in a frame over the fireplace. My mum had asked my grand-father to get rid of it, apparently because she said it upset us kids. That was a blatant lie. We loved that picture and he knew it, so he refused to take it down. Dean was our dad now, and if we had a problem with that we could just shut up about it.

The one exception to all this was Daniel. For some reason my mum accepted that, as the eldest, the death was upsetting for him. As a result, Daniel was always pampered as a victim by her. The more he was pampered and treated as a delicate exception, the more isolated he became from the rest of the family. Daniel developed an extremely bad temper, and he would sometimes flip out completely and beat Michael up. He eventually became seen as the black sheep of the family.

But my stepfather Dean wasn't having any of it. He took Daniel's behaviour and special status as an affront.

'Why is he like that?' he'd continually ask my mum. 'Why are you treating him differently? Why are you're mollycoddling him?'

'I'm not mollycoddling him,' she'd say. 'He's just different from the other boys. He's a sensitive lad. He's got easily hurt feelings. He's not a boy's boy like the others.'

'You're not doing him any favours.'

'It's because of what happened. He just needs bit more care and attention, that's all. He'll be fine.'

But he wasn't fine. As Daniel grew into his teens, my mum still wrapped him up in a special protective cocoon, and as a result his behaviour got worse and worse. In an attempt to toughen him up, Dean made him take up rugby. In the first game Daniel ever played, he managed to get one of his teeth knocked out. From then on, he insisted he didn't want to play any more. Mum stuck up for him and said that was fine. Dean was furious. He was constantly goading him, which caused Mum to wrap him up even more. In the evenings and on long weekend afternoons, Daniel would sit and talk to her for hour after hour. Mum would spoil him too. Anything he wanted she'd make sure he got. When he became a teenager, he started borrowing money off her. He took up listening to heavy metal and grunge, and grew his hair long.

Dean couldn't understand any of it, but my mum wouldn't hear a word against her eldest boy. All of this made Dean feel excluded, ignored and furious, and undermined what he saw as his rightful place at the head of the family. He began to single Daniel out. This, of course, caused Mum to treat Daniel even more as a victim. As the years went by, Daniel and Dean began to absolutely hate each other. This eventually caused an enormous divide in the family that threatened to tear it apart completely. Mum and Dean would have these massive, wall-shaking arguments, to the point where he would leave the house for days on end.

Dean leaving the house didn't bother me. It was more peaceful when he wasn't around. But what was sad was seeing Daniel change from being a normal, happy, healthy older brother to becoming a young man ruined by being repeatedly told he was a victim. Of course, he believed it was true. He felt the pain of missing his father and, rather than accepting it, dealing with it and trying to move on, he was actually rewarded for *not* dealing with it. When he allowed his grief to overwhelm him and make him isolated, and when he took it out on other people, he was lavished not only with motherly attention but with gifts and money.

It all came to a head one winter Sunday, when I was fifteen and Dan was seventeen and a half. The driveway of our house opened out onto a main road that led to the nearby town of Saint-Lô, and when Daniel hit his mid-teens he started to hitchhike out there quite regularly. He'd escape the house to drink and smoke puff and hang around with his French girlfriend. That day, some time in the early afternoon, I remember being up in my room watching MTV when I heard my mum coming noisily into the house, followed by the sound of the kitchen door slamming behind her. She was screaming and crying. I rushed downstairs to find out what was happening. I found her at the kitchen table with her head in her hands.

'What's going on?'

'Daniel's outside, over the road, and he's trying to kill himself,' she said.

'What do you mean trying to kill himself?'

'He's got a pen. He's trying to stab himself with it.'

'Well, stop him! Why aren't you trying to stop him?'

'Just leave him. Just leave him. There's nothing we can do for him now.'

'We can't leave him!'

'I've been out there trying to stop him doing it. It's no good. He's split up with his girlfriend.'

'Well, we've got to try again.'

I made for the kitchen door.

'Anthony, don't you go out there. There's no point.'

'Where the fuck is he? Tell me.'

'I can't look. I've tried. It's too late. Oh, I can't look.'

I could guess exactly where he'd be. Just opposite the house there was a grim little muddy area by the side of the road, where Daniel would stand with his thumb out whenever he tried to hitch into Saint-Lô. I tore out of the kitchen, ran to the end of our drive and jumped over the gate. The road wasn't usually that busy, but when there was traffic it was mostly farm lorries and industrial vehicles travelling fast.

As my feet hit the ground on the other side there happened to be a string of trucks, filled with what looked like potatoes, rattling past. Through the vehicles flashing by I could see my brother on the other side of the road. He was in the Kurt Cobain T-shirt he never seemed to be out of, with his ripped black jeans, his silver pentagon neck chain and his lank hair almost to his shoulders. He had his fountain pen in his hand, his arm was bloody, his face was red and pale and bubbling, and he seemed to be looking intently at the lorries as they passed on my side. He then began looking the other way, down his side of the road. It was empty. What was he doing? Looking for a lift? Looking for more lorries? What the hell was he thinking?

As soon as the going was clear I charged across both carriageways and immediately tried to grab the pen off him. But he was too quick and too determined. He swiped the pen away and dug the nib deep back into his forearm.

'What the fuck are you doing?' I asked, wincing.

'I'm just going to kill myself,' he said. 'It's easier.'

The good news was, in his madness, he'd decided to kill himself with a fountain pen. His arm was a bit of a gory mess but, in all honesty, if the plan was to use that pen to end his life, he might just as well have written a letter to his heart to request it to stop beating.

'Easier than what?' I said. 'Come on, Dan. Just put the pen down and come inside.'

With that, a deep rumbling sound from down the road grew louder and louder. He paused and looked around. It was a huge articulated lorry, this time coming along his side of the carriageway. I'm not sure how – maybe it was a twitch in his stance, maybe that horrible hungry look in his eyes – but I suddenly knew what he was planning. He was going to throw himself under the lorry.

I grabbed him in a bear hug, and he began struggling furiously.

'Don't be so fucking stupid, Dan,' I said. 'We love you. What's wrong with you?'

'Leave me alone,' he said. 'Just fucking leave me.'

The lorry drew closer and closer, the sound of its engine like an angry charging animal coming right at us.

I began choking up. 'Don't be so stupid, Dan. Please, mate. Please. We love you. We all love you.'

There was a pause in his struggling, as tears started pouring down my cheeks. Seeing me in this state seemed to snap him out of it. I loosened my grip a little.

'All right, Ant,' he said. 'I'm not going to do it, I'm not going to do it.'

I let him go and he slumped to his knees. Thank God. But just as the four-foot wheels of the huge rusting lorry were actually bearing down upon us, everything changed. In the space of less than a second I saw Dan fix the lorry in his gaze and tense his body to spring up under its path. Time almost ground to a halt. With all my strength, I leapt on top of him, throwing myself around his neck, his throat gripped in the crook of my arm, my other hand going for the bloody pen. For a moment I wasn't sure what was happening. The sound of the lorry's horn blasted into me, terrifyingly close, vibrating my clothes against my skin. We were moving, tangled up together. Hitting hard ground. Tumbling. Falling. I couldn't see anything. Where were we? Were we under the lorry? Was this it?

We came to a halt at the bottom of an irrigation ditch. With the road clear I let my brother go, then I suddenly became aware of a sharp slicing pain just above my stomach. I looked down and saw that the pen had stabbed into me when I grabbed it.

'Look what you've done,' I said.

Dan looked horrified. 'Mate, are you all right?'

'What does it look like?' I said. 'What are you doing, Dan? You're going to destroy the family if you carry on like this. Stop thinking about yourself for a change and start thinking about the rest of us. Don't you care about us? We love you, Dan.' I motioned towards my bloody belly. 'Look at what you're doing to us.'

With that, he curled himself into a ball and began crying uncontrollably.

We walked together back to the house in silence. I know now that I was lucky his pen stuck into me. I reflect upon its lesson every time I glimpse the scar it left behind. What ended that terrible situation was Daniel seeing that his own actions had physically hurt his little brother. The sight of all that blood jolted him out of his state of miserable self-obsession. For one precious moment Daniel was forced to take a tiny bit of responsibility for his behaviour. He was confronted with the fact that he wasn't the world's only victim. Other people could bleed too. This moment of clarity probably saved his life. But sadly, the clarity wasn't to last long.

Throughout the years he never really broke out of his victim mindset, and I have to confess I'm partly to blame. That incident by the roadside made me fearful that Daniel could make a new attempt on his life whenever things went wrong for him, and after pulling him out of that suicide attempt I felt especially responsible for his well-being. Going through such an intense experience together had somehow given us a bond we hadn't had before.

After I left home and joined the army, he got into the habit of phoning me up whenever he was feeling fragile. 'I need help, mate,' he'd say. 'I'm not really myself. I think I'm going to take a bad turn here.' As soon as I heard that, I'd drop everything and go and stay with him for a weekend or longer. We'd cook together, we'd go out and I'd buy him dinner, then we'd talk long into the night, just as he used to talk to Mum in the kitchen of our childhood home.

At that time he was living in Paris while I was based in Portsmouth, so my trips to take care of him were neither cheap nor straightforward. His girlfriend was working and he wasn't, but he never seemed that motivated to look for a job or keep hold of one when he managed to find work. He didn't seem that bothered about relying on everyone else. He'd become so used to other people looking after him that it had just become the norm. He felt no shame in doing a supermarket shop, with me in tow, and then when we reached the cash register saying, 'I've got no money, mate. Can you sort this out?' I always said yes. When I wasn't around and his girlfriend was skint, he still had my mum at his beck and call. He'd phone her continually and get her to send him money.

After a few years of this, my wife Emilie began pushing back. I was just starting out in the green army and didn't really have the cash or the time to be lavishing it so freely on my needy elder brother. And even if I did, how was it fair, Emilie would ask. She could have enjoyed a nice weekend in Paris instead. Soon the proper arguments started. I told her she was being selfish. Couldn't she see that Daniel's life was in the balance? He was fragile, damaged, different, needed extra care and attention. If I failed to heed his calls, or left him without enough money to get by, there was a strong likelihood he'd wind up dead.

Our worst argument came when she found out that I'd taken out an overdraft in order to send him money. He was staying in a studio flat where the rent was £400, and he'd got himself in arrears. I didn't want to see him being booted out onto the street, so I'd organised a £500 loan and had the funds transferred to his account.

'We're supposed to be having a child,' she said. 'How can we afford to raise a kid if we're in debt?'

As I began defending him, with the same old arguments yet again, I suddenly realised what was happening. History was repeating itself. Exactly the same dynamics that had nearly destroyed the marriage of my mother and stepfather were now threatening to seriously damage ours. I'd simply become a new parent for Daniel, so he had two mothers now. Not only was I completely subservient to him, I was also being ground down with worry, affecting my performance during the day in the army – and my family life. As much as I loved him, it seemed that Daniel had become this centre of negativity that spread out like a poisonous liquid, soaking into everything it touched. But what could I do? My brother's life was in my hands. How could I ever forgive myself if I refused him and he wound up in the River Seine with a paving slab roped around his waist?

The breaking point came soon after that bitter argument with Emilie about the overdraft. I'd only just made up with her when Daniel called yet again.

'Mate, can you sort me out another hundred?'

'What for?' I said. 'Your rent's £400 and I've just given you £500. It's going to be ages until I can pay the bank back.'

'Yeah, thanks, mate,' he said. 'You're a diamond. But there's this gig, this concert. It's just for tickets. Two tickets.'

I couldn't believe what I was hearing. Was he serious?

'Daniel, I've just paid your rent.'

'Yeah, I know. Thanks, mate. But I really want to go to this concert.'

There was a silence.

'You're almost thirty years old,' I said. 'You're my elder brother.'

'What's that got do with anything?'

'I can't keep doing this, Dan. I just can't.'

After that phone call I just went cold on him. When he'd phone me up and ask for help, I'd either not take the call or straightforwardly tell him no. After I'd said no enough times – or simply refused to take his call – he eventually stopped calling. Although he'd still sometimes visit my brother Michael in Portsmouth, he knew not to come to me. I wouldn't fall for his victim card any more. Although I loved him and feared desperately for his future, I had to cut him loose. I had to let him be. He had to figure his own life out for himself. If he was going to kill himself, he was going to kill himself. His life was in his own hands, not mine or my mum's – and that was the way it should be.

Cutting my vulnerable brother loose like this might seem harsh, but how else could I have actually helped him? From the age of eight he'd had a reality created for him to exist within that was wholly negative. My mother had made him a cocoon whereby being completely protected and provided for had simply become normal. Her coddling of him confirmed all his worst fears – the world was full of danger and it was impossible for him to survive in it without heavy protection. That heavy protection caused friction in the family, isolating him from his brothers and making my step-father hate him. Nobody really wanted to be near him, so the family home became a hostile space for him. The effect of that was to seemingly confirm that, yes, the world in general was indeed a highly dangerous place. And that made him crave his security in the victim's cocoon even more – which made my mum give it more, which isolated him more, and so on and so on. It just spiralled down and down.

And now I'd been recruited into the task of maintaining this cocoon for him. Both mum and I were well-meaning – we wanted Dan to be happy, and to live and thrive. But what had we achieved? By telling him that he was a victim and, even more damagingly, treating him like one, that's exactly what he turned into. Whenever he failed to take responsibility for his life we'd reward him – with love, attention and endless cash prizes. This was surely the worst thing we could have done. Rather than encouraging him to deal with the pain of my dad's death in a rational and healthy manner, we motivated him to luxuriate in it. His victimhood became who he was. It became an identity and a lifestyle. In trying to protect him, we'd damaged him. We'd created a thirty-year-old infant.

What other option was there but to break this negative cycle? Daniel had grown into a man who was scared of everything. He was stuck in the same corridor that he'd been in since the age of eight, too scared to open any doors. He couldn't take responsibility for himself because he saw reality as too difficult to cope with. He didn't believe he could do it. The only way to show him that he could open those doors and grow into a man was to force him into it. And that meant cutting him loose.

I last saw Daniel about eight years ago. He invited me, Emilie and the kids out to his house in the middle of some woods. After lunch we were chatting in the kitchen and he broke down in tears. He thanked me for cutting him off. 'It was the best thing you could've done,' he said.

Daniel is a complicated person who's been through a lot. I love him. He's still my elder brother. I heard from him a while back – he was working, going regularly to the gym, and has a wife and three children. He has, finally, become a successful adult.

THE DEFAULT MINDSET

The truth is that most people are a bit like Daniel, if not necessarily as extreme. They see the world as dangerous, threatening and, all too often, overwhelming. Life itself is too much for them to cope with. Why do they think this? Because that's what their brains are constantly telling them. How did their brains become filled with this information? Because that's what they've been told at crucial points in their lives. For the first decade and a half of our existence on earth we're in the care of usually well-meaning parents or teachers. In the modern age, the number one priority of these caregivers is to keep the infants in their care safe from harm. So what do they tell them? 'Be careful.'

Endlessly. Over and over and over again, in different variations. Don't do this, don't go there, don't touch that, stay away from him, leave that alone, make sure you do this, be careful, be careful, be very, very careful. And for sixteen or more years, that information is pouring into the easily influenced young brain from all directions. Parents and teachers exaggerate the dangers of the world out of a sense of misguided love. And what do children do? They believe their parents and teachers. Of course they do. To a child, Mum and Dad are nothing less than gods. As we're growing up and learning about the world, we're constantly being bombarded with signals not only that reality is full of threats and enemies, but that we're powerless in the face of them and have to be on our continual guard.

When we grow into our teenage years and beyond, we're immersed in media that continue to convince us that all this fearful propaganda is true. In order to reap their profits, everything from Hollywood to TV to the newspapers has to spew out endless tales of terror and horror, whether they're of street crime or health crises or terrorism or tornadoes or earthquakes or political instability or war. Never mind that we spend the vast, vast majority of our days in a state of absolute security and safety, taking our kids to school, picking up groceries from the shops, playing in the park on Sunday afternoons. Despite the overwhelming evidence of our safety, the message never ceases that the world is a highly hazardous place and we're no match for it. We fail to realise that this message is false because it's all-pervasive. It utterly surrounds us, literally from the moment we're born. *Be careful!*

But it's incredibly damaging. It helps to form our underlying perspective on the world. Our default mindset becomes one of deep fear, and that fear stops us living the lives we're truly capable of. Many of us spend every day of our earthly existence stuck in that default mindset. The good news is, it's surprisingly easy to snap out of it. I learned this lesson the first time I was in a proper firefight. I was leading a team of men on a mission to go after a Taliban commander who, we'd learned, had only been in the country for a couple of days. We were dropped off some distance away, and walked in to the target in silence. As soon as we got there and the first bullet was fired, all hell broke loose. We call that a 'noisy' operation. We entered the enemy's base and saw at least one enemy combatant run into a room in a central building. I knew that room would be my next target, and I knew it would be extremely dangerous.

I ran up to the door and got into position, with my teammates lined up behind me. Bullets from an AK47 – maybe more than one – started flying out of the door. My fear was immense. That default mindset kicked in, and who could argue with it? The world was undeniably dangerous. I was about to enter a door through which bullets were firing. I had no choice but to do it. The moment the gunman paused, I decided, I would have to get in there and get the drop on him. The bullets stopped. I went to move. I couldn't. What was happening to me? My legs were like concrete. 'Fuck, Ant, get a grip.'

The bullets began firing again. Another pause. But I still couldn't move. I was literally paralysed with fear. Time seemed to halt completely. Fear was swallowing me. My mind was going haywire. The longer I spent in that fear bubble, the more I felt the life draining out of me. Just as I was beginning to convince myself that I was never going to get through that door, my pal behind me reached around and squeezed my shoulder as if to say, 'Don't worry, Ant. When you go through that door I'm right with you.' The moment he did that, I felt limitless. It was as if he'd put a bulletproof shield in front of me. I committed. I went in.

Even in this genuinely fearful situation I was able to switch out of that default 'Be careful' mindset. It starts with clear thinking. That means understanding exactly where the default mindset comes from – all the lessons that those well-meaning parents and teachers gave you when you were a child, all the times they told you 'Be careful' and that the world was too dangerous for you to cope with. And then it's about consciously focusing on the fact that this is categorically not true – even in pretty extreme situations.

I hope and expect that nobody reading this book will ever be in as dangerous a position as I was, stacked up at that door in the midst of my first firefight. It was only natural, then, that because my brain was screaming out *BE CAREFUL* with such incredible ferocity that I was paralysed from the waist down. But what I hope to show is that it's very rare for the default mindset to be at all accurate. What really characterises it is the assumption that everything is going to be the absolute worst-case scenario – that what lies behind any door you're about to step through is the worst possible thing you can imagine. For me, right then, that was a wall of highly armed Taliban fighters who would mow me down in an instant. But when I went in, I found one guy who was even more scared than I was, curled up in a corner, firing bullets chaotically. Yes, I was in danger. But I also had three highly capable men right behind me. This wasn't the worst-case scenario. Even in the midst of a firefight my default mindset was calling it wrong.

Life is full of doors that are a bit like this – but they're doors behind which there are not terrorists but amazing new adventures and opportunities. The default mindset doesn't want you to open them. It wants to keep you in your corridor because it's familiar with where it's already at and knows that you're safe. But you don't have to nod your head like a good boy or girl and accept that mindset. You can throw it off. You can accept that you're not that child any more who needs to be constantly told, 'Be careful.'

CUT NEGATIVE PEOPLE AWAY

If you decide not to throw it off and remain with your default mindset forever, you'll fail to open those doors that life is constantly showing you. You'll stay stuck in the same corridor for year after year. And that corridor is a trap. Because here's the truth that the fearful voice in your head repeating 'Be careful' over and over doesn't want you to know. Staying in that corridor doesn't just mean remaining where you are, being the same person forever. It means you shrink. You get weaker. More pathetic. Fear is a magic shrinking potion. If you don't learn to harness it, it will make you smaller and smaller and smaller.

And yet other people around you, who are actually summoning up the courage to open those doors, will grow. They'll enter their new corridors, and slowly but surely become new and better people. They'll have success. They'll earn money. They'll look better and dress better. They'll probably smile more. And how will you justify your decision not to open those doors and stay exactly where you are? You'll turn the blame around and direct it to those happier people. You'll convince yourself that your failure is somehow their fault and they're all conspiring against you or cheating the system. And you'll also blame the world in general. You'll tell yourself that it's all a fixed game, that there's no point in even trying because everything's set up to make you fail. You'll begin mistaking your fear for wisdom, telling yourself that you're not scared but smart. Leaving those doors closed begins to feel like the only intelligent option. Your mindset has now become negative. You've turned yourself into a victim.

Victimhood is a self-fulfilling prophecy. When you fail to harness your fears and become a negative person, that negativity will rapidly colour your view of everything and everyone. Your brain will spot traps and enemies everywhere. One of the tells that you're in the presence of a negative person is that they often use language in a certain way – they say words like 'always' and 'never' and 'everyone' a lot, because they're continually telling themselves that every situation and every human being they encounter is the same and out to get them. They globalise their negativity because they want to reassure themselves that the problem isn't their own lack of courage, but everyone and everything else.

When you meet these people, they'll want to convince you that their negative worldview is right. So they'll attempt to fill your head with the same thinking, spreading their dark cloud of doom and dread as far and wide as they can. If they're not enjoying their job and failing in their responsibility to sort their professional unhappiness out, they'll be motivated to convince themselves that it's the job that's the source of their problem and not their own lack of courage in fixing it. So they'll bitch and whine about their bosses and the company, and make you feel like a traitor or a naïve idiot if you don't agree with them and refuse to join in.

Likewise, if their relationships with friends and family are not working, and they're failing in their responsibility to make them right, they'll be motivated to want to believe it's the other person that's the problem, so will try to get you to hate them too. If they're envious of other people's success, because they're failing in their responsibility to open their own doors, they'll talk them down, mock them and minimise their achievements. They'll put pressure on you to hate them too.

Not only will negative people try to push their worldview onto other people, they'll try to push their responsibilities onto them as well. They're constantly complaining about this person or that person, keeping a tally of who they believe owes them what, and becoming outraged and offended when someone fails to assist or support them in the way they feel entitled to. Positive thinkers push and change themselves in order to succeed in the world. Negative thinkers want the world, and other people, to change in order to accommodate them.

And what's the end result of this kind of behaviour? Negative people become isolated. The only people who'll want to be anywhere near them are other negative people. All the positivity drains from their lives. They become isolated. Eventually they make true their own horrible fantasy of reality. They actually get the vicious, dangerous world that their minds imagined, surrounded by enemies of their own creation.

Make no mistake, these are powerful forces. Negativity is our default mindset. It comes only too naturally to us. Our brains are built out of those millions of tiny lessons that contained the message 'Be careful' when we were growing up. These same brains are motivated to keep us safe, so they're on high alert for hazards, traps or enemies in the environment. They're naturally always wanting to tip into negativity and have us run to the safety of the back of the cave, especially when we fail in life. It's because of this that when contestants on *SAS: Who Dares Wins* decide to give up and voluntarily withdraw, we get shot of them straight away. They're sent to their accommodation, and are told to pack their bags and get on the next flight home. It sounds harsh, but we simply can't have any negativity seeping out and affecting the others who are still in the game.

If you don't want to become one of these negative people, it's essential that you don't allow people who have such a worldview to become a part of your life. If you do, they will quickly begin to colour your perspective. You'll be likely to find yourself falling for their seductive excuses for fear and failure, and taking on their responsibilities. This will drain you. It will make you more fearful. It will make you smaller. I don't care if they're lifelong friends. I don't care if they're brothers or sisters. Cut them loose. Be brutal. Because they're harming you. I know this is a fact from my own experience. When I was still dashing between Paris and Portsmouth, fretting about Daniel, I became a worse soldier and a worse husband. I was snapping at Emilie and distracted at work. If I'd allowed him to, he would have destroyed everything. I had to assume responsibility for my own life, and let him assume responsibility for his. And that meant cutting him away.

THE UNFORTUNATE RISE OF VICTIM CULTURE

I find it tragic that the victim mindset is currently spreading throughout Western culture like a psychological pandemic. People have found a way of making victimhood work for them, and are broadcasting their messages of complaint and accusation to try to raise themselves up. These people are currently dominating our national conversation. Their worldview is that of the young lad above me on Snowdon who gave up and climbed down. It's the worldview of my elder brother. They look at reality and choose to see only dangers. They blame everyone else for these dangers, persuading other people to make special allowances and alter their behaviour to accommodate their wishes. Sadly, the Daniels of this world are taking over.

I feel the pressure to conform to today's victim culture all the time. These people don't like the fact that a man like me can be happy, successful and positive in my outlook. I've been to war. I've witnessed absolute horrors, men wailing in shock and agony with their own intestines cradled in their arms, and eight-year-olds strapped up with explosives and used as suicide bombers. I've picked up a wig, in a terrorist encampment, only to realise it was a fresh human scalp. I've carried the headless, limbless torso of a fellow Marine onto one stretcher and helped stack his severed body parts onto another. I've committed acts of street violence. I've been kicked out of the police force for drink driving. I've taken steroids. I've lost my father. I've been to prison. And I have not been damaged by any of it. I'm absolutely 100 per cent fine.

In fact, I'm more than fine. I'm loving life. And yet time and time again I'm told, 'But Ant, you can't be fine. You must be damaged. You must be traumatised.'

When I insist I'm not, these people refuse to accept it. 'You've killed people, so you must have suffered,' they say.

'Not at all,' I reply. 'In fact I miss the battlefield almost every day.'

'But how can you live with yourself? People are dead because of you.'

'It was nothing personal. It was what I had to do.'

'Well, there must be something wrong with you, you're just not admitting it. You're out of touch with your emotions. In denial. You're too caught up in your own toxic masculinity.'

I've had conversations along these lines dozens of times, often with journalists or people online. When I don't fit the assumptions of the victim mindset, they first respond with disbelief and then become offended. What's truly sick about all this is that they actually want me to be traumatised. They want me to have nightmares and an alcohol problem. They want me to suffer from PTSD. My life isn't a victim story, and that just doesn't compute with them. They take my happiness and healthiness as a personal insult. I'm continually being given the message that it's not OK to be OK. Well, I'm here to tell you that this is a truly grotesque way of seeing the world. It is diabolical. It condemns positivity and success, and celebrates pain and damage.

But believe me, I do understand how useful the victim mindset can be. Crying 'victim' is the most efficient way of cheating the system. Some time after my arrest for assaulting a police officer, the charges were raised from Actual Bodily Harm to Grievous Bodily Harm because the officer in question claimed he'd suffered permanent damage to his eye. On top of that, I was charged with common assault against a female officer whom I never actually touched. Apparently she 'felt' that her safety was under threat and, in today's victimhood culture, if a person *feels* harmed then they *are* harmed. I'd hoped that I would get away with a fine or a caution, and was surprised that this was actually going to trial.

At one point, however, someone on my team offered me an almost guaranteed way out.

'The reason you flipped out is because of your experience of war,' he said. 'It's as simple as that. It's trauma. PTSD. It simply wouldn't have happened had you not witnessed the horrors of conflict in service to your country. Add in the traumatic loss of your father at a young age, too, and the argument starts to make itself. All you need to do is apologise, talk about your PTSD, get some psychological help, therapy or counselling or whatever, and we can easily make this go away, I'm almost certain of it.'

'Absolutely not,' I said. 'I'm here because I made a bad choice. That's what happened. I wasn't thinking about my father. I wasn't thinking about war. I don't have PTSD.'

'You're not listening,' he said. 'If you've got PTSD, your problems are essentially over.'

'No, *you're* not listening,' I said. 'I haven't got PTSD.'

Despite this apparent opportunity to wriggle out of trouble, I chose to take responsibility for my actions. Although I was hopeful that the judge wouldn't send me to prison, I was willing to take that risk. When he sent me down for fourteen months I didn't regret my decision for an instant. I wasn't the victim of circumstance. This was all my fault. I had made a choice. A bad one. And I would accept the consequences.

It's unfortunate that we live in an age in which my decision might be seen as surprising or unusual. It's as if no one accepts that they should be held accountable for their actions any more. If someone wants to manipulate the system for personal gain, they simply find a way of being a victim. Hard work, grit, determination, brutal honesty, self-accountability – this is the hard way around. This is the route to success that a person can take pride in. Working hard every single day is not easy. Being brutally honest with yourself is not easy. Holding yourself accountable and accepting the consequences of your actions is not easy. But do you know what is easy? Blaming everyone else for your problems.

This kind of negativity can only breed more negativity. If that's your mindset and your focus, then that's who you're going to become. People who are motivated to see the world as made up of competing victim groups are condemned to become the kind of people that they claim to despise. If you decide to view reality as being made up of warring genders, then that's the world your mind will create for you. If you decide to view reality as being made up of warring racial groups, then that world will be created for you. And then what happens? As soon as you're in that world, you'll pick your team. And human minds being human minds, you'll start being biased towards your own team and prejudiced against the other one. You'll start bitching out your rival group, only ever seeing the worst in them. And guess what? Now you've become a sexist. Now you've become a racist. Congratulations. Welcome to victimhood hell.

The truth about victimhood is that everyone has some fact they can point to that 'proves' that life is more difficult for them – I was poor, I was abused, my dad was a drug addict, my mum hit me, I was depressed, I hated my body, I was ugly, I was bullied, I drank too much. The list never ends. What about this one? I, Ant Middleton, am the victim of multiple sexual assaults. I am harassed repeatedly, whenever I make a public appearance. If I had a pound for every time a woman groped me, I'd be able to buy myself a solid gold crown with 'V' for victim picked out on it in rare diamonds and rubies. I'm a married man. Even if I weren't, it's not at all pleasant to be treated like this.

Or how about this one? You might not be aware that there's a well-established prejudice in society against short men. Male leaders in business, politics and the military are significantly taller than average. I, Ant Middleton, am a short man. Of course this isn't one of the fashionable prejudices that receives endless attention in the media or gets government funding and special programmes. But even if it were, I'd never dream of using it as an excuse. Quite the contrary – you use such prejudices as extra motivation. You use them as fuel.

I worry, too, about the effect that victim culture is having on our children. That 'Be careful' message that parents and teachers bombard their kids with as a matter of course has gone haywire. They're being raised in a victimhood culture and it's terrifying for them. By the age of twelve or thirteen they're often suffering from anxiety and depression. We're filling these little minds with fear and negativity. What kind of adults are they going to turn into?

What victimhood culture doesn't comprehend is that you can't remove all conflict and pain from the world. It's simply not possible. There are always going to be winners and losers in life. But in trying to eradicate it from childhood we're failing our kids. It's through conflict and pain that they learn how to deal with conflict and pain. It's how they learn courage. It's how they come to understand that when they do lose, which will inevitably happen, they can pick themselves up, brush themselves off and try to win the next time. It's how they became capable of opening those doors and bursting into new corridors, growing and taking responsibility and becoming better people.

It's important to remember that we don't have to conform to victim culture. We can fight back, allowing our children to be children and our teenagers to be teenagers. We don't have to tread on eggshells whenever we talk. I never go out of my way to offend, but no matter what you say – in this day and age – someone will always be offended. People's offence is their own problem. Whenever I get any negativity over something I've said or done, I usually ignore it. If the people coming at me don't know me, they're not worth my time. Even if it's someone in my inner circle, I don't automatically take it on board. As long as you have the courage to be brutally honest with yourself about your flaws, no kind of verbal abuse ever has the power to knock you over.

HOW TO DEAL WITH NEGATIVE EVENTS WITHOUT SLIPPING INTO VICTIM MODE

No matter what our gender, race or sexuality, we're all going to experience pain and suffering. That's guaranteed. Success is really having the ability not to let fear and negativity rule your life and dictate your mindset. We all encounter enemies. We all take on losses. It's in these periods that we're most vulnerable to slipping into feeling sorry for ourselves, which can lead so naturally into blaming the world in general and turning the whole planet into one huge fear bubble.

The most negative event I've ever had to deal with is the loss of my father. If I'd allowed it to take me over, the anger I felt towards my mum for not letting us mourn him and trying to rob us of his memory would have ruined my life. Although it certainly helped derail it for a few years, I eventually got a grip on myself. These experiences helped me come up with my own process that I now use to deal with negative events in a positive and rational way. It's a simple process, with three steps: acknowledge, process, move on.

1. Acknowledge

Accept that this negative event has happened. Feel the pain of it. Don't resist or deny it. Be brutally honest about your situation, looking at it coldly and rationally, without allowing fear to put you in a state of denial. While I don't forgive my mum, I've had to accept that people sometimes do bad things. She and Dean not only tried to steal his memory from me, they tried to take his London family away from me by forbidding me to contact them. Sadly, when I did finally track down my London family after many years of not seeing them, I discovered that they'd let the situation overwhelm them. They hadn't fully accepted it, and were still

stop something similar happening in the future. This is about possessing the courage to make that harsh acknowledgement about your actions. But don't beat yourself up. Don't enter the corrosive mindset of blame. Fault and blame are components of the victim mindset.

If you can't make it your fault, accept that it is your problem. Own it. My father's death wasn't my fault but it *was* my problem. My feelings around it could only be processed by me. In the case of my brother Daniel, his suicidal behaviour wasn't my fault – but my feelings around his suicidal behaviour *were* my problem. Then ask, what are you going to do about it? What can you do to make sure something like this doesn't happen again?

3. Move on

Once you've acknowledged that the negative event has happened and you've rationally processed it, taking responsibility for what you can and working out what the event isn't, you should soon be able to begin moving on. Moving on healthily and with a positive mindset means not looking back. No bitterness. No vengefulness. No hate.

CHAPTER 5

IN THE FOOTSTEPS OF THE LANKY BEEKEEPER

DEATH LIES SCATTERED about the slopes of Mount Everest like litter. There are more than two hundred dead bodies still up on the mountain, some of them almost perfectly preserved, looking as if the person has decided to just lie down ten minutes ago and take a quick nap. Others are nothing more than piles of bleached bones with rags and strings flying off them. One of the most famous Everest bodies is that of an Indian climber, Tsewang Paljor, whose corpse is often used as a waymarker by climbers. He's known as 'Green Boots', because of his lurid plastic mountaineering boots that still stick out of the nook in which he huddled for shelter back in 1996. Another, Francys Arsentiev, was known as 'Sleeping Beauty' to nine seasons' worth of climbers, until her body was hauled to a quieter spot in 2007. Green Boots and Sleeping Beauty remain in their freezing, earthly heaven, along with all their silent companions, partly because of the sheer cost of their recovery and partly because of its difficulty. It's been estimated that an 80-kilogram human body, when frozen, weighs upwards of 150 kilograms. Unsticking it from its icy tomb and lugging it back down to the foot of the mountain wouldn't only cost tens of thousands of dollars, it would risk yet more lives.

And the corpses come from everywhere. As was evident from that long list of fatalities I'd browsed all those months ago on the train home to Chelmsford, the lure of Everest is powerful enough that it can draw people to it from every corner of the planet. Japan, South Africa, USA, India, Slovakia, Italy, Brazil, Cambodia ... that five-and-a-half-mile-high black and white monster doesn't discriminate on grounds of nationality, nor does it quibble about race, age or gender. Blood tastes like blood to the king of the rocks.

Of all the nations that have taken up its challenge, however, Everest still holds a special place in the heart of the British. The mountain was first identified as the world's highest in 1852 following calculations by an Indian mathematician based on observations made by the British Trigonometrical Survey of India, at a time when it was only known to us as Peak XV. It took a further thirteen years for it to gain its Western name, which was given in honour of the former Surveyor General of India, Sir George Everest. Naturally, as soon as word got out that it was officially the highest, people wanted to climb it. The problem was that the two countries from which the mountain could be reached, Nepal and Tibet, were at that time closed off to outsiders. No serious mountaineer could get near it.

It was only seventy years later that British diplomats managed to gain permission from the Tibetan authorities to launch an attempt on the mountain. With the blessing of the Dalai Lama, the British tried to reach the top with six different expeditions – not counting the two reconnaissance expeditions of 1921 and 1951 to establish which routes of ascent were feasible. All of these attempts to climb the mountain failed, and it was on the second expedition, in 1924, with the tragic disappearances of the glamorous George Mallory and his companion Andrew Irvine, that the quest for the summit turned into a national obsession.

After the Second World War, national pressure to bag the summit became even more intense. Tibet was invaded by China, which refused permission for any more attempts from the northern side. Towards the end of the war, a series of secret reconnaissance flights of the mountain had been carried out by British pilots flying Spitfires and Mosquitos. They brought back detailed photographs showing a possible route from the Nepalese side to the south.

Then, in 1949, after centuries of isolation, this previously sealed kingdom started opening up to foreigners. In the autumn of 1951 the Nepalese authorities gave permission for Eric Shipton, known as 'Mr Everest' because of his repeated attempts on the mountain in the 1930s, to lead a reconnaissance mission up through the Khumbu. With the Sherpa Tenzing Norgay, Shipton was the first to navigate a way up the fearsome Khumbu Icefall as part of a seven-man team, and he returned convinced that a route to the summit could be made from the south. The intelligence he gathered on this trip was to prove critical to every subsequent expedition from the Nepalese side. And if that wasn't enough, he also brought back photographs of huge, mysterious footprints that, it was widely speculated, belonged to the legendary Yeti.

The news that there was a feasible way up the mountain's Nepalese side sent reverberations around the world's elite climbing communities. And then the shocking news was announced. The Nepalese authorities had finally granted permission for an attempt to be made on Chomolungma's summit – to the Swiss. Not only had another nation been given a fair shot at what Britons had come to see as their own mountain, it had been given to a mountain people with alpine climbing in their blood. Britain held its breath as the Swiss expedition made its assault in 1952 … and then turned back after reaching 8,595 metres on the south-east ridge, the normal route from the south used today. This was a relief, but only a temporary one. They'd not claimed the summit, but they had set a new altitude record for climbing. It was now just a matter of time. The next British expedition was due on the slopes the following spring. The year after that, the French were going. The year after that, it was the Swiss again. For the British, it was now or never.

Most expected Mr Everest to be given the job of expedition leader. But on 11 September 1952 a telegram was thrust into the hands of a colonel in the British Army called John Hunt, inviting him to take on the role. When he read the message, as he recalled in *The Ascent of Everest*, 'I experienced excitement and apprehension in more or less equal proportions.' He went about recruiting a team of climbers between the ages of twenty-three and forty-three, describing one of these men, somewhat unpromisingly, as 'lanky in build; by profession a bee-keeper near Auckland'. This was Edmund Hillary. What was appealing about Hillary to Hunt was not so much his physical build and climbing prowess – although he was obviously an experienced mountaineer in his home country of New Zealand – as his positive mindset. Hillary was, remembered Hunt, 'abounding in a restless energy, possessed of a thrusting mind which swept aside all unproved obstacles'.

On 12 February 1953 the main expedition sailed out of Tilbury in Essex, just half an hour's drive from my house. When the team reached Kathmandu, where there were no hotels, they were put up by the British ambassador. Although lead Sherpa Tenzing Norgay was offered a bed, the other Sherpas were made to sleep on the floor in the garage, and they registered their fury by pissing over the embassy walls. By the time the party reached the Khumbu they were being assisted by twenty Sherpas and 350 porters, carrying three tonnes of equipment between them. The first summit attempt was made on 26 May by Tom Bourdillon and Charles Evans. They faltered just 100 metres from the top, and their names are now almost entirely forgotten. Three days later it was the turn of Hillary and Norgay.

Having feasted the previous night on sardines on biscuits and tinned apricots that they'd had to thaw out over a Primus gas stove, and after a fitful sleep in temperatures that dropped to $-27°C$, they woke at 4 a.m., downed 'large quantities' of lemon juice and sugar, finished off the last of their sardines and were away by 6.30. All went well until, just shy of 29,000 feet, they encountered 'the most formidable problem' – a forty-foot rock step that was 'smooth and almost holdless ... a barrier [it was] beyond our feeble strength to overcome'.

But Hillary, with his positive mindset, refused to accept defeat. On the step's east side he found a small face of rock split by a deep, narrow crack that ran up its entire length. He jammed himself into it – 'taking advantage of every little rock hold and all the force of knee, shoulder and arms I could muster, I literally cramponed backwards up the crack.' This steep expanse of rock is known as the Hillary Step, and everyone with ambitions to reach the top from the south has no choice but to scale it. I would soon come to know its dangers all too well.

At 11.30 a.m. on 29 May Hillary became the first person to stand on the summit of Mount Everest, followed closely by his partner Norgay. 'There was no disguising his infectious grin of pure delight as he looked all around him,' Hillary recounted later. 'We shook hands and then Tenzing threw his arm around my shoulder and we thumped each other on the back until we were almost breathless.' Tenzing made an offering to the gods, burying a bar of chocolate, a packet of biscuits and a few lollies in the snow. Next to these gifts Hillary buried a small crucifix. After a brief hunt for signs of Mallory and Irving, they left the top of the world. Hillary's first words, on returning to camp, were to his friend George Lowe: 'Well, George, we knocked the bastard off.'

The next day they descended to Camp IV – much lower down the mountain than the modern camp of that name – where the main party was waiting, and gave them the news, with George Lowe signalling their victory by thrusting his ice axe wildly towards the summit. As expedition leader John Hunt was to recall, 'Everyone was pouring out of the tents; there were shouts of acclamation and joy. The next moment I was with them: handshakes – even, I blush to say, hugs – for the triumphant pair.' From there, the *Times* journalist James Morris rushed down to Base Camp, where he recruited a porter to run to the nearest town with a message that read: 'Snow conditions bad stop advanced base abandoned yesterday stop awaiting improvement.' This message was then transmitted to the British Embassy in Kathmandu, from where it was wired to London.

'Snow conditions bad' was code for 'Summit achieved'. The incredible news was finally released on 2 June, the morning of the coronation of Queen Elizabeth II. As the expedition turned on the radio in their tent at Base Camp after their evening meal, they heard the crackling announcement from back home: 'The wonderful news broke in London last night that Everest has been climbed by a British expedition.' Hunt ordered up a jar of rum for the men. 'There would be many more to follow,' he wrote.

WHAT WITH ALL this history bound up with my mission, I was excited to finally reach Base Camp and see it for myself, although I wasn't expecting it to be a pretty place. That *Times* journalist who accompanied the 1953 British Expedition described it as 'too dead and aloof for beauty, rather as if some dread disease had passed this way, killing everything in sight, to be followed by some giant instrument of hygiene, so that the place seemed to have been effectively murdered, and then sterilised'. Eloquent, but perhaps a bit harsh.

To be fair, however, he wasn't all that far off, although much about the place had changed in the intervening sixty-plus years. Base Camp was a tented village lying at an altitude of 5,335 metres at the snout of the glacier that rolled down from the vast ice fields of the Western Cwm above us. By now a universe away from the meadows and fields of the lower Khumbu, we were surrounded by high serrated walls and peaks, their black pinnacles and flanks mostly coated with snow. The valley floor looked to be nothing more than a great dump of boulders and rocks with no flat ground anywhere, and blue and yellow tents seemingly randomly pitched, as if tossed by a careless giant. The only decorations were the long streams of prayer flags that had been strung here and there, and the glorious blue dome of the cloudless Himalayan sky.

Because we were here so early in the climbing season it was still relatively quiet. There were probably about five hundred people in camp in total, but they were mostly staff preparing for the influx of expeditions, when over a thousand bodies would fill this otherwise lifeless place, each one requiring hot food and drink, a warm place to sleep – and many of them wanting it in all the luxury they could afford. There was an almost constant stream of Sherpas, porters and kitchen staff coming in, with people bringing in new dumps of supplies every day. There was even a helicopter landing pad.

Base Camp was the ultimate destination for the most hardy of the tourist trekkers, and they'd often stay only one night. You couldn't blame them for wanting to go back down as soon as possible. It wasn't only that the camp wasn't pretty; it was also dangerous. Just two years earlier an avalanche struck this place, killing eighteen people. Despite the partying trekkers there was now a noticeably more serious atmosphere, and above here it would be climbers only. It was a major psychological gear change from everything that had preceded it on the trek in.

All the tents were actually organised in huddles, belying their random appearance, so that each expedition company had its own small area. As soon as I could I located Madison Mountaineering's camp and found my two-man tent. I crawled in, laid out a couple of roll matts on which I put a pillow and a huge, thick yak blanket I'd bought along the trail, then laid my sleeping bag on top of it. After that, I set about getting all my kit squared away. I was going to be spending a total of around four weeks in this little tent, so I wanted to make it feel like home.

That evening, over mugs of steaming tea, I had a long chat with Dawa.

'I live for the seasons,' he told me.

'What do you do with yourself for the rest of the year?'

'Sometimes training. I've just returned from Switzerland. Next I want to learn Long Line Rescue. When I have enough saved.'

'You train in Switzerland?' I said. 'How much does something like that cost?'

'Oh, a lot, a lot, a lot,' he smiled. 'Perhaps $5,000, perhaps more. I don't know. But I like to do it. It's an investment in my life. It makes me better.'

'Tell you what,' I said. 'Instead of giving you a $1,000 summit tip, what if I pay for you to do that?'

For a moment he looked speechless. He was about to speak, but I cut him off.

'Don't thank me, Dawa,' I said. 'Not yet. You've got to get me up there first.'

And so began the rest period, during which I was to take it easy and allow my body to become used to operating in this oxygen-deprived air. I was just beginning to get into the groove of spending some downtime with Ed and Dawa when, to my disappointment, some of the other Madison clients began to trickle in, having had the time to catch us up. One of them was a millionaire from America – let's call him Ferris. Although he was in his early thirties, he looked and held himself like a bratty school kid. When I'd met some of the other members of the Madison expedition back in Lukla, I'd immediately become wary of this guy. A sense of fuck-you entitlement radiated off him.

My impression of him didn't improve when, just before leaving Lukla, Madison's clients gathered at the place where our kit was being stored, ready for collection by the Sherpas who'd haul it up the mountain.

I was just leaving the unit when Ferris strode in with one of the Sherpas and pointed to his load. 'That's mine, that over there, that green one. That red one, you see that one? And that other red one, with the poles strapped onto it? And this yellow one is fucking super fragile so do not, whatever you do, subject it to any kind of rough handling. That's extremely important.'

As he was talking, I could tell his Sherpa was still trying to process what he'd just heard.

'So which of these bags are you taking?'

'Which ones?' he said, with a passive–aggressive smile. 'All of them. The ones I've pointed to. They're all mine. They're all coming up. That's not going to be a problem, is it?'

Curious, I peered over the Sherpa's shoulder and surveyed his load. It was as if he was going on a holiday. There were spare boots, spare trekking poles, a spare ice axe, bunches of carabiners. He had spares of spares of spares. God knows what was in the rest of the bags. I was told later on that his Sherpa had to lug four *extra* bags up the mountain for him.

I took a step back and put a friendly hand on his shoulder. 'Fucking hell,' I said. 'What, are you having a party up there?'

An expression of flustered, defensive confusion came over him. 'Yeah, but you never know.'

On my third evening at Base Camp I heard someone bedding in to the tent next door. He had a hard, dull cough, and it seemed clear that he was already suffering badly from the altitude. I was trying to rest, although it was proving hard with the endless hacking. Every now and then I'd hear the zip of his tent open, followed by the sound of him throatily spitting out a mouthful of head-gunk. Eventually, he seemed to get a handle on it and his coughing became less persistent.

But as I started to nod off I heard some bizarre rhythmic sounds wafting in on the breeze. Was I dreaming? Was it the alarm on my clock or something? I pushed myself up on my hands and focused in on it. No, there is was – dibbetty-bib-betty-doooo … dibbetty-bibbetty-doooo … di-di-di-di-di-di-dibbetty-bibbetty-doooo. It was that idiot next door. I couldn't believe it. He was playing a computer game. Of course, I soon realised that the idiot was Ferris. He'd had his Sherpa drag a computer up to Base Camp for him. The next morning, at first light, I stumbled out of my tent to find myself nearly stepping in all the pools of blood-laced phlegm that he'd coughed up and were now frozen to the rocks like so many icy pink jellyfish.

People like this were dangerous and they didn't belong on the mountain. Later on, during the trip, I'd make friends with someone who had an inside track on what was going on with Ferris. The idea was for the expedition to move as one group from camp to camp, up and down, as they all completed rotations, acclimatising and practising techniques together. But Ferris quickly fell behind everyone else and showed no apparent interest in catching up. Soon he was lagging behind by eighteen hours. There were only two Western guides available to lead everyone, but now one of them was obliged to remain at his side.

His slowness wasn't only due to his altitude sickness. It mostly seemed to be because he was so embarrassingly unprepared. He couldn't ice climb. One day some members of the main Madison group did a bit of training on an icefall a short walk from camp. Everyone had got up it, but he was still there, right at the bottom, having spent thirty minutes simply trying to work out how to kick his feet into the ice. All this wouldn't have been so bad if he'd cared about the impact he was having on everyone else. But he refused to acknowledge that his behaviour was detrimental to the group, and he had no respect for the team or anyone else. 'We really need to try and catch up,' a Western guide said to him at one point, to which he apparently replied, 'Don't forget, I'm your client.'

After Madison's main expedition left for Camp II, Ferris had to stay back at Camp I. By then he was in absolute rag order, almost constantly coughing up blood. When he was advised to descend to Base Camp, he refused point blank. His attitude was, 'I've paid my money, I'm your damned client, you do what I say.' People like this think they can buy the mountain. It never occurs to them that they have to earn it. Like the classic victim, they want everyone else to bend and change in order to accommodate their weaknesses.

It was just such a mindset that contributed to the disaster on Everest in 1996. During the second week of May the track to the summit had become choked up with so many climbers that bottlenecks had formed at both the Hillary Step and a small ledge known as the Balcony.

Strict instructions for the climbers to turn around by 2 p.m. if they hadn't reached the summit were ignored. Several high-paying clients insisted they must summit and Western guides submitted to their wishes ('I didn't feel comfortable telling clients who'd paid $65,000 that they had to go down,' said one). Then a blizzard blew in. Eight people died, including two highly experienced expedition leaders, Rob Hall and Scott Fischer. It was during this blizzard that Green Boots met his fate.

At the root of this buy-the-mountain attitude is an unwillingness to take personal responsibility. People like Ferris don't hold themselves accountable for anything. Later in the expedition, when a group of them were at Base Camp waiting for a helicopter, Ferris was still wearing his ceremonial cloth kata that had been draped around his neck following his blessing by the lama. As the helicopter came in to land, the kata was sucked into its blades. The damage something like that can cause could easily have taken the helicopter down and put it out for the season. Everyone else, of course, had tucked their katas in. His immediate reaction was to blame someone else. 'Well, *I* didn't put it round my neck,' he said. 'The Sherpas did it.' It wasn't long before the rest of the expedition began avoiding Ferris. Nobody wanted to be around him.

Lying there in my tent in Base Camp that night, I could still only guess how much of a problem Ferris would eventually prove to be to everyone else in his group. I hoped I'd left the idiots behind back on the trekking trail, yet here was one in the tent right next to me. As I drifted off to sleep, a sense of dismay enveloped me. I'd come for an adventure. I'd come for fear. But maybe this trip would turn out to be exactly what I'd told Emilie it was. An expensive camping holiday.

During the night I felt the ground moaning, cracking and creaking as the glacier shifted and stretched. Some time before dawn I was suddenly woken by a huge cracking sound. I bolted upright. What was that? The noise was coming from right underneath me. It was in the ground. Then, suddenly, it was all around me. The cracking rose in volume to become a roar. I flung myself to the edge of my tent and yanked down my zip. This was an avalanche and it was coming straight for us.

'Fucking hell, Ant,' I muttered. 'What have you got yourself into?'

CHAPTER 6

THE FEAR OF SUFFERING

AS I SCRAMBLED for the zip of my tent that night, the intense feeling I was experiencing was one of the most fundamental varieties of fear. I was scared that I was going to be buried under tonnes of ice and would freeze or suffocate or be left alone to endure the agony of a dozen broken bones. This was the fear of suffering.

The fear of suffering is a constant. It's an ordinary part of the daily life of everything on the planet that has breath. I wouldn't be surprised if humans suffer from this variety of fear more than most other living things, simply because we have such incredibly powerful brains. We have detailed memories of past events, which means that experiences of physical and mental pain and suffering can linger in our heads for years and come back to haunt us, provoked sometimes by only the slightest trigger. We also have incredible imaginations that we use to predict the future. When it looks like something bad is going to happen to us, such as being crushed beneath an avalanche on Mount Everest, a combination of the memory of past experiences of pain and the imagination of what's about to happen enables us to vividly imagine all the agony that's about to hit us. Add in the default mindset that's always expecting the worst-case scenario, and you have the perfect recipe for crippling fear.

I've seen the fear of suffering nearly overwhelm my children. And, in carefully working out how to help them through it, I've managed to learn some lessons that anyone can apply. When my son Gabriel was eight, we entered him into his first Mai Thai competition. He was going to be competing in an inter-club match, Chelmsford versus Romford, in front of a large audience of parents and other young fighters. Emilie and I discussed the fight, and we decided that I would take him and she would stay at home. Experience told us that if his mum was there with him he tended to cry a lot when he had to spar, whereas if I took him he always wanted to prove himself by being a tough lad.

'He just needs to get in there and get the job done,' said Emilie. 'If I go he'll blub.'

As soon as we turned up on the day of the match, I could tell that Gabriel was becoming anxious. We walked through the door of the Romford gym to see rows of seats arranged around a large ring in the middle of the room. We signed him in, had him weighed to make sure he'd be fighting someone who was roughly the same size, and then handed in his medical form to confirm he was fit and able. Following all that, we were given a rough timing of when his turn to fight would be. It was bad news. He'd been assigned a match at the end of the day. That meant three or four hours of watching people get hurt.

Just as I'd feared, as the morning kicked in and the fighting kicked off, Gabriel turned suspiciously quiet.

'Are you all right, son?' I said.

'Dad,' he replied, looking up at me, 'I don't really want to fight.'

'Look, son. Get it into your head, you're fighting.' I motioned towards the workout area in the corner. 'Go over to the pads with your trainer and start warming up. Don't knacker yourself out, but get your heart pumping. Get into your headspace.'

Of course, the point of the warming up wasn't to make his fear go away. That wouldn't have been possible. Instead I was hoping that the physical activity, and his acceptance of what was going to happen, would help to harness his fear and turn it into the right kind of aggressive energy. I wanted his fear to become a driving force rather than a crippling one. And it seemed to work for a while. But by lunchtime he'd just been in his fear bubble for too long. He was becoming drained. When the fighting recommenced for the afternoon bouts and one young lad in the ring took a hefty hoof to the ribs, my son started crying.

Crying has evolved for a reason. It's nature's way of manipulating other people into trying to get them to help you out or let you off. Used at the right time, it's a kind of weapon. In this particular instance it was Gabriel's way of trying to manipulate his dad into telling him, 'You're all right, son, you don't have to open this door.' As weapons go, crying is an incredibly powerful one. You'd have to be a pretty hard-hearted bastard to watch someone in genuine tears and not feel a thing. The moment I see anyone cry, whether it's a man, woman or child, I flip into a different mode. The vast majority of us do. That's why the weapon is so effective.

But there was no way I was going to allow my son to cry his way out of this fear bubble. He'd been doing Mai Thai for nearly a year. He loved the sport. I had no doubt that he was capable of performing that day. So what was I going to do?

THE 'GET READY' RESPONSE

The answer began with taking a step back and reassessing the fundamentals. Asking the question, what is fear anyway? Fear is what happens when your brain perceives that a challenging situation is likely to happen to you at some point in the future. The closer that point in time gets, and the more challenging the potential situation, the greater the feeling of fear. Scientists have pinpointed the region in the brain that's largely responsible for processing fear. It's called the amygdala. Whenever a threat is detected, the amygdala triggers a cascade of processes to prepare for what's about to happen, including a sudden rush of hormones that flood the body – our heart rate and blood pressure go up, we start sweating to keep cool, our digestion slows so that our resources are preserved and we enter a state of psychological alertness. This is the famous fight-or-flight response. It's the mind and body's way of getting us ready for whatever potential trouble has been clocked on the horizon.

With all this in mind, I decided to ask Gabriel exactly what he was feeling.

'I don't want to fight,' he said once again.

'No, "I don't want to fight" is what you're thinking,' I told him. 'I asked what you were feeling.'

'Scared.'

'That's a nice try, mate,' I replied. 'But it's still not what I want to hear. Tell me how you're feeling in your stomach.'

'A bit sick.'

'Yeah, you're getting there. Describe to me what your stomach feels like.'

'Heavy.'

'That's right,' I said. 'That's actually what you're feeling. You've got a heavy stomach. Now tell me what your skin feels like.'

'Cold and sweaty.'

'Exactly. And can you feel your heart right now?'

'It's beating.'

'Is it beating harder than normal?'

He nodded.

'Get ready. Can you feel it? Your body is getting ready. It wants to go.'

With that, he jumped into the ring, gave out a couple of valiant kicks, got punched in the face and burst into tears. But rather than quit, he carried on. When the round was over, I took myself over to his corner and gave him a little coaching.

'Wipe the tears, son,' I said. 'When you cry he can see that there's weakness there. You'll give him the upper hand. Now, come on. Feel it. Your body is pumping you up. Get ready.'

Despite his distress, he strode back into the ring in control of his fear. And then *he* made *his* opponent cry.

Three rounds later, the match ended in a draw. It wasn't the perfect Hollywood ending I'd have liked to tell you about, with the crowds going crazy and Gabriel being held aloft by adoring fans, but he did seem to come out of that experience a different boy – more confident, more in charge, raring to go in for his next tournament. When that tournament came around, however, he was exactly the same again, crying and doubtful. That was all right. I knew I wasn't going to transform my boy in one day. But I also knew that the more he practised, the more he'd learn that the default-mindset voice in his head – the chatter that was telling him he was going to get paralysed or have his spine snapped – was to be ignored.

What I wasn't telling him was that he would never be hurt in a Mai Thai match. Of course he was going to be hurt.

You're never going to get out of any kind of fight pain-free. But the lesson was, that's OK. Being hurt isn't the end of the world. It usually doesn't mean all the things that that default mindset chatter is telling you. It means nothing more than being a bit sore and swollen for a couple of days. The ultimate goal is for Gabriel to be hurt in the ring and yet not be that bothered by it – to learn the potential, reality and limitations of his own body. I want him in the ring thinking, 'Come on, I can take much more than that.' But he'll never get there if I allow him to listen to the chatter. At the end of the day, it's going to take raw experience to really prove to him that the voice in his head is a liar and that fear itself is nothing more than a feeling of 'Get ready'.

'GO' OR 'NO'

I've since found that an understanding of the 'Get ready' response is a brilliantly effective technique for popping fear bubbles. It works because it allows you to redefine fear. When you step into that bubble and experience those intense emotions and thoughts rushing into you, you can now separate them out. The trick is to put your panicky thoughts to one side. Ignore that chatter. Understand it for what it actually is – nothing more than the bubbling bullshit of the default mindset, your brain's over-protective mother on overdrive. Focus solely on the feelings. Don't deny them.

should find these experiences become progressively easier. This isn't only because you're making use of my methods. It's because you're painstakingly showing your own brain that the worst-case scenario it keeps predicting just isn't going to happen. Just as my son needed to teach his own mind that he wasn't going to have his spine snapped and his kneecaps popped out every time he stepped in the ring, so you need to teach yours that the suffering it's dreading and expecting is probably just a fantasy, and that when you do feel even severe pain it's not the end of the world. It's just another feeling that eventually passes.

GET READY TO HARNESS FEAR

By practising these techniques you'll soon be able to begin using the awesome power of fear to your advantage. If you train yourself to experience fear as your body saying 'Get ready', rather than it being a destabilising experience, the fierce, rushing energy that possesses you when you step into your bubble can ultimately make you feel as if you've got jet engines strapped to your legs.

But beware. Just because you've managed to harness fear, it doesn't mean it's automatically under your control. Like an amateur jockey on a thoroughbred racehorse, you still need to learn how to control it. Anybody who's served in the military has heard the horror stories of what can happen when soldiers get swept up in their fear. Although they can use it as an energy, to power them from bad situation to bad situation, when they fail to control it and it begins controlling them, terrible things can happen.

I still have a vivid memory of the time I realised I'd learned not only to harness my fear but to keep it under my control. We were in the battlefield, seeking the hard arrest of a terrorist who'd recently taken out four Marines by hiding explosives in a wheelbarrow and making a child push it towards them before blowing the whole thing up. Hearing that story during the briefing, I was already finding it hard to prevent waves of negative emotion from overcoming me.

My job was to take out the sentry who was guarding the base where this man was staying. But when I arrived at the correct location, the sentry seemed to have vanished. I crept up to the corner where he was supposed to be stationed thinking, 'Where the hell is he?' There was nobody there. Surrounding the base was a low, ruined wall. I peered over it. Empty. What was going on? Had the enemy been tipped off? Did they know we were coming?

Gingerly, and with my weapon ready, I stepped over the courtyard wall. And trod right on the sentry. A jolt of fright bolted through me as the man, who'd been sleeping or hiding, leapt up with a shout, only for the entire place to erupt. As three or four enemy combatants began shooting at us, I rode the relentless waves of my fight-or-flight response, allowing them to lift me into a place of peak awareness and performance. My team and I fanned out and began dealing with the job at hand, and, as we did, out of the corner of my eye I saw a figure jump up, run into a one-storey building and slam the door shut behind him. That would have to be my next target.

I ran up to the door and took my position against it. My arms and legs were shaking. I was at a code red level of fear and anger. I took a fraction of a second to harness their power and kicked the door. That's when I really knew I was on the verge of losing control. The thing practically exploded off its hinges. I entered the room and ran into my drills. The place seemed to be empty except for an object in the corner. There was what looked like a table with a large cloth draped over it. I grabbed the object and threw it to the middle of the room. As soon as I touched the thing, it moved. I watched it fall with a dense thud on the dusty floor. I stood over him, my trigger arm shaking, and just about to pull the trigger. And that's when I realised I was looking at a twelve-year-old boy. My immediate response was to take my finger off the trigger. My first thought was, 'How can I protect this child?' That's when I really knew I'd learned the skill of both harnessing and then controlling my fear.

CHAPTER 7

THE ICEFALL

WE WERE LUCKY. The avalanche that was coming for us petered out just before it reached our camp and, miraculously, none of the Sherpas that were working in the icefall were injured. But there was no doubt it came close.

I spent the next few hours tossing and turning in my tent. Getting any solid, restorative sleep in that place took a bit of practice, even when you weren't woken by the roar of thousands of tonnes of snow and ice coming at you. For a while it had seemed almost impossible to find a flat surface to stretch out on. It was surprisingly disorientating, finding myself waking up in a completely different position to the one in which I'd fallen asleep because the glacier was moving beneath me. And it was cold. My sleeping bag could go down to −20°C, but in the −10°C of our position, 5,335 metres up Mount Everest, it still felt pretty chilly. I'd gaze upwards trying not to think about the fact that, higher up the slope, temperatures could drop to −40°C and ten feet of snow could fall in a single day.

But after another night or two of getting used to it, it all became easier and I started to get some proper rest. Despite the looming dangers up on the icefall, after a week in Base Camp I felt more than ready to tackle it. I'd spent a lot of time working on my acclimatisation, taking mini hikes along small trails, trying to get used to being physically active at that altitude. At the beginning, every single footstep I made was a huge effort. I'd take two or three steps and have to stop to recover. The higher I climbed along the training trails, the more I felt the need to rest. Even though I was doing next to nothing, it was as if my body had to constantly keep reminding itself to breathe. In, out, in, out, every breath an effort.

Apart from that there was nothing much to do in the vicinity of Base Camp except for sitting in the mess tent, chatting with the others, while the Sherpa cooks dished up heavy but welcome and tasty meals of meat, rice and potatoes. In the days following the avalanche the mood around camp had become noticeably more tense. Thankfully nobody was hurt this time, but it had been close. Many of the local guys had friends and colleagues among the fourteen men who had been killed in the incident two years before, and the events of the early morning were an unwelcome and pretty menacing reminder of their loss. On the anniversary of the disaster the Sherpas led a minute's silence in commemoration of the dead, and everyone gathered together in prayer.

'How do you feel about things like that?' Ed asked me, as they were setting their ceremony up.

'Yeah, do your minute's silence and your mark of respect,' I said with a shrug. 'But it just puts you in that negative mindset. I don't ever like to go into that mindset myself because it can be a dark place. It brings back memories of my father, memories of people I've served with who are buried.'

I obviously kept my behaviour respectful but the truth was that I wanted to be a million miles away from all the negativity. If you thought about death and the dangers too much, the fear of suffering would swallow you up and you wouldn't get out of your tent. This is exactly what happened to a few of the people on our expedition. The group would gather in all their kit, ready to go at the appointed hour, and some of them simply wouldn't be there. Never mind that they'd spent $100,000 or more on their challenge of a life-time. Sometimes it was the bitter cold and their exhaustion that started affecting them, sometimes it was the dawning realisation of what they'd got themselves into and the fear that comes with that, sometimes they'd have a near-accident that would send their minds spiralling.

That was the big one. If you have a bad time on the mountain, even lower down the slopes, it can get into your head very quickly. People make the mistake of focusing on the dangers. But all you get from entering that negative thought process is a hundred new reasons to be scared. Your psychological chatter goes into overdrive. I heard some of them talking about Green Boots and Sleeping Beauty, and they were wondering if it might end up being them. But those were other people's decisions that happened on other days. This is a new day. These are your decisions. The avalanches that are set off in your head can be as bad as the ones on the hill. Once you start doubting and become Mr or Mrs Maybe, it's all over.

The night after the avalanche, regardless of the dangers and their own troubled memories of friends now gone, the brave Sherpa fixing team went back up into the icefall to continue their essential work. They were active at night because that's when conditions are safest. Although it never stops descending the mountain, the ice moves with greater speed when the sun is up and radiating its heat all across the icefall's length. It's then that the ice loosens – seracs the size of tower blocks are more likely to crack, topple over and smash into the icefall, while seemingly bottomless new crevasses can open up. Not only that, but the heat that radiates off the white surfaces can become unbearable to work in. It can actually get boiling hot up there.

Every evening we were in Base Camp, Ed, Dawa and I would sit outside in cheap camping chairs, sipping hot tea and watching the tiny pinpricks of light from the fixing team's headtorches seemingly miles in the distance moving slowly up and ahead as they felt out a new route, put in ice screws and fastened ropes for the new season's climbers to ascend. They seemed unbelievably remote and fragile up there, like tiny bugs picking their way up the body of a monster. We had to be patient – we'd be stuck there at Base Camp until they finished.

A couple of days before we were finally able to ascend the icefall ourselves, Ed popped his head into my tent.

'Hey, mate,' he said. 'I'm going to go and practise a bit of ice climbing. Come along.'

It had been years since I'd done any ice climbing, so what Ed proposed was a good idea. Practice was exactly what I needed. But something gave me pause. What was really going on?

I couldn't help but feel that part of the reason that Ed was asking was because he remained unconvinced that I was up to the challenge of Everest. His suggestion wasn't about helping me out as much as it was about checking me out. I suspected he was testing me, perhaps even wanting to put me in a position where he'd be helping me and I'd be asking for his advice. I instinctively reared back. I wasn't going to give that to him. No way.

'You're all right, mate,' I said. 'I'm just going to chill back here for a bit.'

After he left, the situation began gnawing at me. I lay there in a mild hypoxic trance, watching the pattern of the wind as it played roughly and noisily with the roof of my tent. Back in Lukla, Ed had asked me how high I'd ever climbed. I told him the truth – 6,100 metres up Aconcagua in Argentina. It's known as the 'Mountain of Death' in South America and is the continent's highest peak. That sounds impressive to most people, but I knew I wasn't going to get this one past him. Aconcagua is known as an 'easy peak' among professional climbers and it only kills three people a year. That wasn't all – I didn't even manage to get to the top. The party I was in turned back just under a thousand vertical metres away from victory. 'I didn't summit because we only had one window and the weather was too bad,' I'd told him, but at least he had the good manners to act impressed.

It wasn't that I didn't like Ed. He was proving to be good company and acting like a total professional. But I knew why friction was developing between us. The problem was that he just didn't appreciate someone like me tipping up on his mountain and telling him what to do. I'd come into his world and he was having to adhere to my rhythms – it was a situation that was obviously going to grind on him, so I didn't hold it against him for a moment.

I understood Ed because I was like him. It wasn't personal, it was nature. We were two alphas and were just acting as alphas do. I'd had years of experience working with these kinds of people in the military, not least the Special Forces, which is pretty much entirely made up of alpha males. The difference, however, is that the military hierarchy is closely defined. Everyone knows precisely where they sit on the ladder and what their responsibilities in any given operation are. But out here on the mountain, both of our positions were more ambiguous. And that was making things complicated.

I turned over in my sleeping bag. A lump I was sure that hadn't been there before jabbed into my upper ribs. 'Shit,' I thought, 'I should be out there training with Ed. But I can't have anyone telling me what to do. This is my expedition.'

Later that day it became clear that Ed realised there was more to my refusal to join him than a simple desire to chill. When I bumped into him in the mess tent in the evening, he pressed me on what had happened.

'Why didn't you want to go out?' he asked. 'It was great. You can never have enough practice. I'm telling you, that icefall is a tricky bastard. Even the pros don't like it. Even the Sherpas. I think you're mad. You should have come along.'

I nodded flatly. I didn't have any comeback to that at all.

'I'm chilled,' I said, looking away. 'I'm happy.'

'Are you sure you're all right, Ant?'

'Yes, mate,' I said. 'Don't you worry about me. I'm fine. Believe me. Just make sure you're ready to capture everything when we're up on that icefall.'

The next day I quietly grabbed Dawa and took him off to a twenty-foot wall of ice a short distance from camp, where we practised hard. There was a part of me that actually wasn't too concerned about the fact that in less than twenty-four hours I'd be negotiating one of the most feared and deadly places in all of mountaineering, a world of moving ice that killed experienced climbers most years – and I hadn't actually done any ice climbing for more than two decades. I enjoyed putting pressure on myself. I wanted to feel that fear. That was why I was on the mountain in the first place. But there was putting pressure on yourself and there was being irresponsibly foolish. What was the point in placing myself in undue danger? Plus, quite aside from the danger to my life, there was the equally fearful danger that my lack of practice would show me up in front of Ed. I could not allow that to happen.

With our practice over, I returned to my tent and made final preparations for the climb. I was beginning to feel anxious. As I packed, I gave myself a little pep talk. 'Fucking hell, why are you fearful now?' I said. 'You're safe, you're warm, you've got a flask of hot coffee that you're about to sit down and enjoy. The fear is on that icefall. That's where the bubble is. There's no bubble in this tent.' Soon, thankfully, the distraction of all the practical tasks I had to complete did away with that attack of nerves. At just gone half past midnight I climbed out of my tent, zipped the door up behind me and stepped out into the night.

It was freezing. I'd deliberately dressed so that I'd start off cold, knowing that my body was going to be working hard and I didn't want to be stopping all the time, removing layers and packing them away. On top of my boxer shorts I had thick walking trousers, with my heavy boots over a pair of thick socks; for my upper body I had an underlayer, a mid-layer and a zippy fleece with its hood pulled up. Hanging off my day sack I had a couple of ice screws, a harness, a couple of carabiners (D-shaped metal loops that clip onto climbing ropes), two belay devices (for descending ropes, and which act as friction brakes) and finally my jumar (this also clips onto a climbing rope and helps you ascend – it can move up the rope with you as you climb, but it doesn't slip down).

With my breath billowing out into the dark, thin air, I took the opportunity to sort myself out in the Base Camp latrine – a plastic barrel to which a toilet seat had been attached – in a small tent a short walk from the main habitation zone. The only nods to civilisation were pots of hand gel and rough, cheap toilet roll. I'd heard a few of the people in camp complaining about it, but I'd shat in a million worse places than this.

By 12.45 a.m. I was in our little expedition's prearranged meeting point with my helmet on, my backpack ready and my torch in hand. I immediately realised that my mood of excitement wasn't completely shared by the others. Ed and Dawa, it turned out, were still feeling edgy after the avalanche twenty-four hours earlier. It turned out that one of the Sherpas who'd been caught up in it was Dawa's father. A chunk of ice the size of a large room had taken out all of his ladders and he'd fallen more than twenty feet. He was one of four of Madison's Sherpas who'd had to be rescued that night and it had understandably left Dawa pretty freaked out.

'Is he all right now?' I asked Dawa.

'He is shaken,' he said. 'I have also heard about another incident the night before. A part of the icefall collapsed. It broke away under the feet of two Sherpas. They fell a long, long way. They're OK, but it was close.'

'Do you think we're OK to go now?' I said. 'Are you happy?'

'I think it is OK,' said Dawa. 'I don't see it as too much of a problem.'

But I could tell that Dawa was worried. His usual cheerful enthusiasm had vanished. Ed, too, looked as if he'd be happy to call it off and do the icefall another night, putting a bit of time between us and the near-deadly drama. I could sense that all it would take for us to postpone the ascent of the icefall was the slightest nod from me. They were waiting for it. I was glad I'd remained in psychological control of the expedition, as if I hadn't the decision would have been out of my hands. And I was determined to get ahead. If we hung around any longer, we'd be joined by the rest of the Madison expedition. I didn't want to be caught up with that crowd of Mr and Mrs Maybes. In fact, I was determined to hit the summit at the earliest opportunity – the very first hour that it was humanly possible.

Before we left, however, there was one final, crucial formality to complete. We had to ask Chomolungma's permission to climb her. This meant taking part in an ancient Buddhist ritual – the puja. Dawa led us to a squarish stone monument built of pale grey rocks. A yellow skirt of material had been attached to its top, giving it a rim of vivid colour. Flags flapped off the top, and gifts of beer, tsampa and popcorn had been left on it, all gifts to the mountain god. At the base of the monument was a brick wall with space for a fire in its middle. Dawa bent down to light it up and then ignite what looked like joss sticks or juniper twigs, which quickly began streaming out a sweet scent. Several Sherpas then gathered with handfuls of rice to sprinkle on the statues of gods to 'feed' them. I walked with them as we paced leftwards around the monument, throwing rice towards it with our right hands, as Dawa murmured and chanted in prayer.

It was essential that Ed and I took part in this ancient ritual, because refusing to do so was thought to be enough to bring bad luck onto the entire group. But even if it hadn't been expected of me, I still would have wanted to join in. I don't possess any particular spiritual beliefs but in that moment I decided to believe exactly what they did. I wanted to enter deeply into the Sherpa mindset. The ritual of the puja left me feeling strangely calm and undeniably ready. At last we were on.

The base of the Khumbu Icefall was barely fifty metres away from camp. We trudged there in silence and took the first steps of our eight-hour mission to Camp I, which lay at an altitude of 6,100 metres. This would be a battle on multiple fronts. The effects of altitude and the lack of oxygen in the air meant that we'd not really felt much like eating, and we'd also grown used to having constant dense, knotty headaches. Then there was the fear. As we disappeared into the vast labyrinth of ice, following the still-fresh trail that the Sherpa fixing team had laid out, we heard the icefall groaning and cracking around us. Chomolungma was alive, its stomach growling. As I began the arduous work of climbing it, it soon began to feel as if I was having a relationship with a person. You had to move with her, roll with her – less like an assault than a seduction. The spiritual beliefs of the Sherpa now made perfect intuitive sense.

Making our way up the maze of grit and ice I found myself losing track of time, an astronaut lost on a faraway planet of endless night. Ahead of me was Dawa, while Ed followed behind me. It was eerie and surreal, as if we'd been swallowed and disappeared down the throat of the universe. Nobody spoke. There were only the sounds of the beast's belly, intimidating in volume. Eventually, after walking for perhaps forty-five minutes, we hit a point where we had to climb. Still in tense, tired silence, we attached the sharp metal spikes of our crampons onto our boots. In front of us was an ice wall, a single ladder leading up to it. Above the ladder, a rope.

Suddenly it hit me. Fear. I found myself thinking, 'What if I can't do this? It's possible I'll fail right here. I'm not ready for this. If these guys knew how little preparation I'd done, they'd freak out. What if my body cannot physically manage the climb?' This was the moment that my trip truly stopped feeling like an adventure holiday.

I had to get a grip on myself. If I watered that seed it would destroy me. 'Fucking come on, Ant,' I told myself. 'You're not even in the bubble yet. Don't quit before you get there. There are going to be multiple bubbles over the next seven hours. You're not going to quit before even entering the first one.' I visualised the bubble at the base of the ladder. 'Just admit you're scared. Acknowledge it. There's nothing wrong with walking into the bubble, stepping out of it and then taking a breath,' I told myself. 'Take small steps.'

I breathed deeply, walked into the bubble and felt the fear rush into me like floodwater. Steady. Steady. That was it. Feel it. Acknowledge it. It's happening. Yes, I could deal with this. That rushing, rising sensation was simply my body telling me: 'Get ready.' And then, I committed. 'Go.' I put one spiked boot onto that rickety-looking ladder and took a step upwards. The fear turned to focused determination. The ladder transformed from a death trap to a helper, each rung feeling secure. Minutes later, I was up.

The relief wasn't to last long. I was still feeling the aftermath of the adrenaline rush when we crossed a ridge and reached our first crevasse, a twenty-foot gash in the ground so deep it might as well have been endless, easily big enough to swallow a hundred men whole and digest them too. We crossed crevasses on the same rickety metal ladders that we climbed up the seracs, but these were laid flat and lashed together with rope. This one was a two-ladder job. Getting to the other side meant walking across it, step by step, trying not to let your crampon spikes get caught in the rungs and trip you up. The only things to hold on to were two semi-taut ropes strung out on either side.

This time I was ready. I took a physical step back from it and summoned up the bubble. It was there, right on the icy ledge, eight foot high and eight foot round, just where the end of the ladder had been dug into the ground. The fear was inside the bubble. I could see it, filling it up like liquid fire. But this time I was in control. I felt calm. The fear was over there – in a different place and a different time to me.

OK. Now.

I took a breath and stepped inside the bubble. The fear poured into me like lava. I felt myself rocking back on my heels. This was a big one. My emotions began to go haywire. They were hitting me hard with those two animalistic options – fight or flight. I knew exactly what I had to do. Leave myself with no choice. These situations were almost easier in a war zone because there the option is actually fight or die. Here I could choose going back down to bed. My tent was only an hour and a bit away. We could have another crack at this tomorrow.

No. Not tomorrow.

For a moment I thought the fear was going to be too much. I knew, from bitter experience, that if you made the mistake of staying in that bubble for too long it would drain the life out of you. You've got to be in it and then pop it as quickly as you can. Only then can you use it properly to propel you onwards, to the next bubble. Fear is a resource, and so is the adrenaline that follows. There was no way I was going to waste it. I had to commit. I would commit. Decide. Make the free choice.

Compose yourself, Ant. Feel that fear. It's real. You're in it. Acknowledge it. Acknowledge the situation.

Get ready.

Go.

And I was on it. I stepped onto the ladder, lifted the guide ropes up, took one faltering step and then the next. I looked down into the crevasse and saw that it was never-ending. Every instinct in me told me to look up and ahead, but I had no choice because I was negotiating the rungs, trying desperately not to catch my crampons on them. All the while the light from the headtorch on my helmet was shining on nothing. It was an absolute abyss, and I had nothing but two lengths of rope keeping me upright. Because the ropes had slack in them when I picked them up, I had to lean into them to get the tension I needed to control my progress with my hands. This meant I was tilted forwards as I went. Every cell in my body was telling me not to put too much downward pressure on the ladder, not to look down and not to lean forwards. Every movement that felt unnatural and unsafe was being forced upon me.

As soon as I stepped off the ladder at the other end, more adrenaline blasted into me. I knew to take this surge of positive energy wisely and let it power me on. I shuffled up past Dawa and took my turn leading the group. We crossed one crevasse and then another. We scaled sheer walls of ice. Before each challenge I went through the process of visualising my bubbles. While they take a minute or two to describe for you here on the page, in real life I usually get through them in seconds. But as one hour turned into two and two hours became three, the adrenaline began wearing me down. Some of the ladders that crossed the crevasses looked highly unstable, especially where the ice had moved from when the fixing team had been there to do their work a night or two earlier and they'd become twisted, refusing to lie flat. Sometimes you'd have to cross one ladder to clear the crevasse, sometimes two; and occasionally my heart would drop at the sight of three of them strapped together with rope. I'd get myself safely across, turn a corner, and there would be another yawning black crevasse and yet another ladder or two. 'For fuck's sake!' I'd think. 'Already?'

Just before dawn I was climbing up a steep ladder when my helmet struck an overhang and the GoPro camera that was strapped to it fell off. It didn't make a sound as it tumbled away, instantly vanishing into the abyss. When I got to the top, Ed did not look happy.

'What happened?' he said.

'It's one of those things,' I said. 'It doesn't matter.'

'There's loads of footage on that camera. It's my responsibility to make the best film possible and I need those shots of you going through the icefall from your point of view.'

'We'll get more,' I said.

'We need to go down and get it. We can abseil down. It's not that far.'

'It's not worth it, Ed. It's gone. Let's go.'

'Yeah, but –'

'Don't let it affect you. There's nothing you can do. It's a black hole. You've got footage. There's a camera in your hand, isn't there? Guys, I'm not joking. We need to speed up. I don't want to be here when the sun hits the ice.'

From there on we shifted up a gear. In order to make it through the icefall as quickly as possible, I began cutting corners and Ed kept trying to correct me. He was getting relentless.

At the base of one ice climb I heard him shout, 'When you get up there, Ant, clip in your safety before you get your jumar off.'

He was right. That's what I should do.

'No, I don't need to,' I shouted back. 'I'll just hold on to the rope. I'll clip on after.'

As the temperature crept up, I took my helmet off to cool myself down.

'Ant, you should keep that helmet on.'

'No, mate. I'll wear a helmet if I need it.'

I tried not to let these little power tussles get to me as we negotiated the rest of the icefall. Instead, I used the emotions they were whipping up in me as fuel. I'd show him I'd earned my place on this mountain through my ability. Eventually he'd get it. I sped on and, finally, after one of the most arduous nights of my life, we finally exited the icefall and found ourselves rubbing our eyes at the foot of the impossibly massive canyon that is the Western Cwm. We'd only just beaten sunrise.

We were beginning to feel the elation of our achievement when we heard an enormous crack, as if the mountain itself had ruptured, the sound bouncing about the walls of the valley. We instinctively ducked, then tried to find its source, but the echo made this nearly impossible. There was suddenly movement. An explosion of snow the size of a football stadium blasted off the side of the mountain as if triggered by some nuclear bomb. This was a big one.

We watched it pile down the slope to exactly where we'd been only minutes earlier, ploughing through everything. As it crashed on its way, it showered us in a fine sheen of snow. It was pure luck that we weren't in it. Surely people were dead. I looked around to see that Ed had turned his camera on me.

'Ant, ten minutes ago that was us,' he said.

I knew what he wanted. I was supposed to act freaked out in front of the camera and play it up.

'Yeah, but it wasn't, was it?' I said.

'Yeah, but I was just saying that ten minutes ago it was,' he said.

'That's your luck, isn't it? Don't think about it.'

The moment you start thinking negatively like that, you're screwed. Why think it could have been us? It had happened over there. We were here. It wasn't us. Don't think about what could have happened or what should have happened. Don't be guided by that 'Be careful' voice in your head. Think about reality. And the reality is, we were fine.

CHAPTER 8

THE FEAR OF FAILURE

IF IT WAS the fear of suffering that was crippling so many of the men and women whom I met on Mount Everest, with their jabbering about Green Boots and their doubts about themselves on the icefall, then another, different form of fear was actually helping them get up the mountain. This is the second of the big three fears that needs to be explored and explained so that it can be harnessed. It's the fear of failure. Just like the fear of suffering, the fear of failure has its own quirks and peculiarities. But what really marks this fear out from the others is the fact that it can be an incredible motivator. More than any of the other varieties of fear, if you learn to properly harness and control the fear of failure it can be your best friend in moments of severe anxiety and dread. It will be there to serve you in many of your most desperate moments.

I've no doubt that pretty much everyone who's ever climbed Everest has used this fear to their benefit at some point. The fear of what their friends and associates back home would say about them if they returned having not reached the summit will have got hundreds if not thousands of heavy legs to keep on moving up the Western Cwm. But, make no mistake, if you don't learn to properly harness the fear of failure it can also be your worst enemy. It can cripple you. Allowed to run rampant, it can ultimately become an excuse not to live, preventing you from blasting through those doors that everyday life offers you and from reaching new, exciting corridors. It can coat your boots with glue and stick you to the floor.

HOW THE FEAR OF FAILURE CAN GIVE YOU STICKY BOOTS

And this can happen to anyone, up to and including some of the most respected men in the military, including Marines and Paras who are at the top of their game, as I know from my own experience. Soon after you join your unit, you find out who they are, these 'legends' who instantly command respect and attention wherever they go. The occasion of my arrival at 40 Commando headquarters in Taunton as a newly minted, freshly passed-out Marine was no exception. The morning me and the other lads tipped up at the base, we were directed to a large brick building where we were told to report to the regimental sergeant major, who would assign us to our units.

Along with the rest of the new intake, I trotted up the stairs and waited in a line outside the RSM's office. One by one the adjutant called us in. Before long it was my turn. 'Middleton!' The adjutant opened the door, and I marched in and stood to attention. There was the RSM, sitting behind his large, immaculately tidy desk with its gold plaque. He was wearing his khaki jacket, shirt and tie, and a shiny black belt was strapped around his waist. Hanging from a hook behind him was his ceremonial cane with its polished silver top cap.

'Marine Middleton,' I said, announcing myself crisply. 'P0636.'

The RSM looked down his list. When he found my name he gave a little grunt.

'Middleton,' he said. 'Welcome to the unit. Right, you've done the easy part. This is where the hard work begins. Report to the sergeant major of Bravo Company. Happy?'

'Yes, sir.'

After the sergeant major had assigned me to 3 Troop, I went to the accommodation and introduced myself to the lads, who seemed like a decent bunch. That weekend we all went out as a big crew to the local pubs that were scattered around Taunton. It's on these beery nights out that you start hearing about the legends of the troop. Stories circulate, over the pool table and next to the cigarette machine – this guy is a sniper, that guy is a Recce Troop operator, this guy served in Iraq, that guy in Afghanistan. But troop gossip isn't the only way to identify the elite. You can spot them by the way they carry themselves and by the little posse of fans that tends to clot around them whenever possible. And that night, sure enough, I immediately spotted the Troop Daddy. He was up at the bar, with four or five shorter guys in his thrall. The bear roar of his throaty laughter rolled over the noise of the jukebox and the chinking glasses.

'Who's that guy?' I asked the lad I was playing pool with.

'You don't know who that is?' he grinned. 'Fucking hell. He's in Sniper Troop. The top sniper in the unit. He was in Iraq. Two tours. That guy is an absolute sniping legend.'

'What's his name?'

'Bench.'

I looked over at the man again. He certainly was a big lad.

'Why's he called Bench?' I asked. 'Is it Bench as in "bench press"?'

'Bench as in homeless,' he replied. 'He used to sleep on one.'

'Oh, right.'

'Aye, he's a tough bastard. He's lived. There's no fucking about with that lad. Proper legend.'

As one of the new intake, I was too lowly for a man of Bench's stature to take much notice of. But I was certainly aware of him as he strode around 40 Commando, trailing a wake of admiration behind him. A couple of months later, however, he passed by me and noticed that I had my parachute wings stitched on to my right shoulder. This obviously confused him. As a Marine, there are two ways of earning your wings. You either complete the sniper course or you pass 'Recce Selection' and become a member of the Reconnaissance Troop, a highly specialised unit that goes behind enemy lines to gather intelligence. Either achievement enables you to go on your 'jumps course' and earn your parachute wings. But I was relatively new around there. A young lad. How could it be that I was swanning around 40 Commando with a set of wings on my shoulder?

'Hey, mate,' said Bench, blocking my path and motioning at the wings. 'So, er, what are you then? Recce Troop? Or Sniper Troop?'

'No, no, I'm just in Bravo Company,' I said. 'I've just got in.'

'But you've got your wings?'

'I'm ex-Parachute Squadron.'

Bench nodded silently, evidently impressed.

'What's your name?'

'Middleton. Ant.'

'Well, Middleton Ant, I reckon you should go on Recce Selection. Man like you. Yeah, get yourself into Recce Troop. You'd be a good fit in there.'

Bench thought he was paying me a compliment. And he was, to be fair. But I had other plans.

'To be honest, I want to do Special Forces Selection,' I said.

A dismissive smirk made its way across his huge, paving-slab face.

'What, you want to do Special Forces Selection? Are you being serious? You've only been here a couple of minutes. Special Forces Selection?'

'Well, yeah. I think so. I really want to go into the Special Forces, so I thought, you know, I might as well just bypass all of that other stuff.'

He shoved his tongue into his cheek and rapidly shook his head.

'Listen, you may have been in the green army, mate, but this is the fucking Marines. This is the SBS we're talking about. If I was you I'd definitely go for Sniper Troop or Recce Troop.'

This was getting awkward.

'Yeah, totally,' I said. 'I do know what you're saying. But you've done a couple of tours already. You're a sniper. Why don't you go on Special Forces Selection?'

'What?' he laughed. 'When I can go to Iraq right now and dust cunts off like that?' He clicked his fingers. 'Fucking … I mean, I've got the perfect job, mate. I joined to be a sniper, mate. I don't wanna be just some silly fucking door-kicker. I mean, Jesus … And I don't know why you're so fucking keen. Do you know what the failure rate is on Special Forces Selection? Something like 95 per cent. You need to chill your boots. Maybe give it five or six years, get yourself in Recce Troop and then have a think about it.'

Like all the other lads my age in 40 Commando, I was in awe of Bench. And it was for this reason that I couldn't wrap my head around what he'd told me. I'd always assumed it was every elite soldier's dream to be in the Special Forces. Obviously not. It seemed pretty clear he was happy with his lot. I knew enough about sniping to know that it was akin to a fine art. It takes skill, strategy and intelligence, and I could quite imagine how, once you'd mastered it, you'd develop a passion for it. So fair enough. For a while I stopped thinking about joining the Special Forces. Maybe I was getting ahead of myself. It seemed smarter to follow Bench's advice. I'd probably join Recce Troop and take things more gradually. Maybe, like him, I'd realise that the Special Forces weren't all that special after all.

Two months or so later I caught up with my sergeant major, who knew of my former dreams of becoming an SBS operator.

'I spoke to Bench and he said I should do Recce Selection,' I said. 'He didn't see the Special Forces as a good idea.'

'He didn't see the Special Forces as a good idea?'

'Yes, sir.'

'Is that what he told you?'

'Yes, sir. So I'm going to give it a few years and then work out if it's right for me.'

'And did Bench also tell you that he put in for Special Forces Selection three years ago?'

'No, sir. He didn't.'

'Which means, in that case, that he didn't also tell you that he withdrew from Special Forces Selection at the last minute.'

'Withdrew?'

'Bottled it. Blew it out of his little squeaky arsehole. Listen. Bench is Bench. He likes to be king of his castle. He's happy where he is. So don't pay too much heed to his career advice. You've got bigger castles to conquer.'

This was a huge epiphany for me. In that moment I realised I was surrounded by these self-made legends in the military, many of whom were actually scared. They'd achieved some success and earned the respect of the people immediately around them, and then become so worried about losing what they had that they stopped opening new doors. They were afraid that they might fail at something, perhaps for the first time in their lives. They were frightened of what everyone else might think of them. They were tin gods, terrified of failure, whose lives had plateaued. The fear of failure had given them sticky boots. They were stuck.

SCARED OF OTHER PEOPLE'S THOUGHTS

Some of the best soldiers I know won't go on Selection simply because of what other people will think of them if they fail. This is a sign that they're being motivated by the wrong forces. I'm going to have a lot more to say about ego versus pride in the next two chapters, but the subject is also highly relevant to Bench's story. His reluctance to go in for

Special Forces Selection told me that his primary motivation was ego. He wanted to succeed in life, mainly because he wanted other people to think that he was something special.

But the better motivation is pride. People who are motivated by pride do things for reasons that are internal not external – they want to impress themselves, not other people. Pride is about testing yourself and pushing yourself. Ego is about getting the adulation of others. The simple fact is, no matter who you are, every human life is full of failure. For the egotist, this means life is full of pain. But for the healthily prideful person, there's not really any such thing as failure. Instead there are only learning experiences.

I learned this truth during the darkest period in my life, when I was sent to prison. The biggest fear I have is failing as a father. During my sentence I had to deal with the fact that as a result of my own bad choices I was no longer able to provide for my family. Even worse, I'd become a burden to them. I was taking away resources from my wife and children, and, in their place, providing massive new stress. What good was I to anyone? Although I felt I didn't *belong* in prison, I knew I deserved to be there. As I stood outside my cell for my first roll call, I could see there was no positive to this situation. I had failed. Massively. Completely. Irreversibly.

Or had I?

It certainly seemed that way. Everything in my situation was telling me that I was a failure. The judge told me I was when he passed his sentence, telling me, 'You should know better, you're an elite soldier.' Being locked up every night, queueing up for my food that was slopped onto a dented steel tray, was telling me I was a failure. Mopping floors all day was telling me I was a failure. Being a number and not a name was telling me I was a failure. Pretty much all of reality was in agreement. I was a failure. And how could I argue with reality?

I could argue with it by realising that I didn't have to let my situation dictate what I believed about myself. It didn't matter what appeared to be true. I was going to decide what was true about myself. I had failed, no doubt about it. But was I going to be a failure? That all depended on how I responded in that moment. Being a failure is allowing your mistake to win. You might have been failing in your life – for the last two weeks, two months, two years, two decades. But you're only a 'failure' for the time that you're allowing that mistake to win. It's simple. As soon as you stop failing, you stop being a failure.

I don't care what you've done or where you've been. Society wants to put you in a box and categorise you. 'You've been to prison,' they say. 'You're nothing but a fucking criminal. You beat up a police officer. How can you strut about lecturing us about leadership and positivity?'

I realise people think that and would like me to accept their thoughts about me as my truth, but I choose to rebel against them. The drug addict in the cell next to me who was still injecting heroin when he was in prison – that was what a failure looked like. He was failing. I had stopped.

When you're motivated by ego, you're allowing other people to tell you what to believe about yourself. Bench tried to do that to me. And it worked, for a while. He looked at me like a kid. He was categorising me. Everyone you know will want to categorise you all the time – as a loser, a failure, a bullshitter, an egotist, whatever. And it's so easy to become that person. But you don't have to let others define who you are. The only time you can truly categorise someone as a failure is when they're lying on their deathbed, leaving a trail of misery and dependency in their wake. That's a failure. A failed person at the failed end of a failed life. Most of us aren't like that. I don't believe that you're like that. I don't buy the idea that you're a failure. You might have failed in your past. You might be failing now. But don't let anyone try to convince you that you're a failure until you're actually lying on that deathbed.

Not letting anyone else define who you are is about being unafraid of what other people think of you. Fear of failure, when it comes from a place of ego, is a fear of other people's thoughts – and why would you be scared of thoughts?

HOW THE FEAR OF FAILURE CREATES A VICTIM MINDSET

But many people *are* scared of the thoughts of other people. Not only does this fear prevent them from learning and growing and smashing into new corridors, it also curses them with a victim mindset. A classic example of precisely this was examined in brutal detail in my TV show *Mutiny*, in which I re-created the journey of Captain William Bligh and his men, after they'd been thrown off their ship HMS *Bounty* and were left to fend for themselves in the wilds of the Pacific Ocean. One of the nine men who was to share the basic sailing boat with me, and who was to become a star of the show for all the wrong reasons, was a young Liverpudlian named Chris Jacks.

Chris was a self-taught sailor who in 2016 had managed to navigate around mainland Britain. He was one of three crew members, along with Freddy Benjafield and Conrad Humphreys, selected specifically for their experience on the water. Because we were trying to closely re-create the conditions of the original 1789 journey, we chose not to use modern technology such as GPS. Back in Captain Bligh's day they relied on a sextant and charts to navigate, but of course none of us were savvy with the complexities of sextant use, so we'd all had to learn and practise with one before the voyage.

Once we'd set sail I began to rely quite a bit on Freddy, a young sailor who'd grown up on a boat with his Royal Navy doctor father and who worked as a skipper for a luxury yacht company. I'd get Freddy to take sextant readings at midday, when the sun was at its highest point. Whenever it was mooted that Chris might take a reading he somehow got out of it. We began to suspect that he didn't actually know how to use a sextant. This was disappointing, but it wasn't the end of the world. I told him, 'Mate, if you need help, let us know. Fred will teach you.' He failed to take up the offer.

I had my suspicions as to why. Chris's nose was already out of joint because I was the captain, Conrad was my first mate and Fred was my second mate – he came third on the list. Chris was a man who put himself on a pedestal. He was the sailor extraordinaire. That was his identity and it was how he expected to be treated at all times. His sense of security, happiness and personal success seemed to rely entirely on other people treating him as the best sailor in the room. He was obviously capable, but by putting himself in this egotistical position he'd made himself vulnerable. It meant that he'd have to cover up or avoid any situation in which he might come across as anything less than perfect.

And Chris was not perfect. Far from it. Instead of acknowledging that he had a weakness and accepting the offer to learn how to use the sextant, he lied and insisted that he knew already. So I decided to test him. I left Chris for his four-hour shift and asked him to take the midday reading. When I returned, I checked in the captain's log to see where we were. And lo and behold, there was no location reading listed for midday. When I asked him what had happened, he told me that he hadn't taken a reading because whoever had last used the sextant had set it up wrongly.

This made zero sense. There's no 'setting up' of the sextant. It was as if I'd given him a Rubik's Cube to solve and he'd said he couldn't complete it because it hadn't been set up properly. It was a comment that betrayed what everyone else already strongly suspected.

'Chris,' I said, 'do you know how to use it?'

'Course I fucking do.'

'Come up and show me then,' I said. 'Show me how to use it.'

He took it off me and started using it. Upside down. The whole crew began laughing at him.

'You're treating me like a kid and belittling me,' he said. 'I'm sick of this.'

If you're someone with a crippling fear of failure, this is exactly the situation you have nightmares about – being surrounded by your peers who are mocking you in unison. And what had made this waking nightmare come alive for him? His fear of failure. Chris was too afraid to speak up. Why? Because his mindset was such that telling us that he didn't know how to use a sextant was the same as admitting that he wasn't a sailor. But he was a sailor. We all knew he was a sailor. He was letting his mistake – not learning sailing like everyone else – define him. He was thinking, 'If I can't use the sextant I'm a failure.' But this was never true.

A part of Chris's weakness came from the fact that he'd taught himself how to sail. When you're self-taught, you're in a little world of your own making. You've never really been through the experience of being judged by other people who know what they're talking about. In Chris's little bubble he was the best in the world. That was his mistake.

Now, at this point, you'd be forgiven for thinking, 'Hang on a minute, Ant, isn't that a positive mindset? Isn't that exactly what I'm supposed to be teaching myself?' But the problem with Chris's mindset was that it was motivated by ego rather than pride. Success isn't simply about getting the badge – 'I'm a sailor'; 'I'm in the Special Forces'; 'I've summited Everest' – it's about earning your place on the sea, in the unit, up the mountain. It's about meeting failure, falling down, learning how to pick yourself up and moving forwards. It's about earning all those scars and calluses that ultimately make you stronger. People like Chris and Bench simply want the badge. They're not motivated by healthy pride. They're less interested in bettering themselves and more interested in wearing the badge. They want *other people* to think better of them even if, in their own minds, they know the less flattering truth. They avoid failure through fear of it, and then crown themselves the kings of their imaginary kingdoms.

Because they kid themselves that they really are masters of their domain, when they're presented with evidence of their failures they blame other people. Turning the spotlight onto themselves would be too painful. Because they're motivated by ego, they cannot do it. So, like Chris, they tell themselves that the problem is everyone else. It's not that you failed to learn the sextant, it's that everyone is belittling you and treating you as a child. Or, in the case of Bench, the problem isn't that he hasn't got the courage to enter Special Forces Selection, it's that the Special Forces are just a bunch of 'silly fucking door-kickers'. This is how the fear of failure can push you into a negative mindset. This is how it can make you think like a victim.

But just because Chris failed in that particular moment doesn't mean he was a failure. There are two potential versions of Chris. The first is the young man that I actually met who wants everyone to think he's this genius sailor, and that's his most important goal. The second one is the man I hope Chris learns to become – a man who just wants to become a better sailor and a better sailor and a better sailor still. This is the Chris who will be ready and capable of enduring multiple difficult failures. This is the Chris who, when given the opportunity to learn from people like Conrad and Fred, will gratefully embrace it. This is the Chris in possession of a healthy, positive mindset.

This Chris will understand a truth that so many of us struggle to grasp. A lot of people fear that if they openly admit their weaknesses, everyone else will say that they're a failure and isolate them. This, in my experience, is absolutely not true. When you admit your fears and vulnerabilities in a positive, optimistic, non-self-pitying way, everyone else will usually warm to you. They'll want to help you. They'll be motivated to pull you into the fold and then take pride in sorting you out.

And what if this doesn't happen? Then you'll know you're in the presence of seriously negative people. It's a signal that you'll need to be seeking help elsewhere. If you accept and acknowledge your weaknesses, and other people mock you for them or use them against you, then get shot of these people. Cut them out of your life. It'll be the best decision you'll ever make. Admitting your failures is the best way I know of finding out who's on your team – and who's not.

YOUR IDENTITY IS YOURS TO DEFINE

Here's where I add a big 'but'. I do understand that nobody's perfect. It's easy enough to say that we should be motivated by pride and not ego, and it's a brilliant ideal to aim towards. But I get it. It's not always possible. The brutally honest truth is that it's often a massive struggle for me. And, to be honest, if I could press a button and flip myself into 'healthy pride' mode forever, I'm not sure I'd press it. In times of great stress, ego can be an amazing drill sergeant. Imagining what people will say about you if you don't pop that fear bubble and burst through a new door of opportunity can often be the final push you need in order to do it. But the important thing is to keep in control of ego. Recruit it as an ally. Put a harness around the fear of failure and let it blast you to your destination.

But go easy. Make sure that ego is working for you, not against you. And, should you fail, flip that failure back into positivity. Flip back to a mindset of healthy pride. And don't be like Chris or Bench and make your entire sense of self-worth dependent on success in one small field. Don't be like that boxer who was once the best in the world, then lost one match and psychologically crumbled, thinking, 'Who am I now?' If this sounds like you, it means you've put your identity in the hands of other people. If you do this, you'll never be successful, because 'success' is not a place that exists in the real world. Success is a feeling. No matter how successful you become, there are always going to be people that somehow want to class you as a failure. In fact, I'd go further. The more successful you become, the *more* people are going to want to class you negatively. If you let them do so, you'll always suffer from some form of impostor syndrome, secretly feeling like a failure even as you're being congratulated on your promotion or picking up the keys to your new car.

The irony is, the people who are defining you as a failure when things don't go to plan are all too often the ones who are stuck in their own restricted corridors. Their fear of being the target of exactly the abuse they dish out has given them sticky boots. Their lives have become frozen. It may well appear as if they're not failing – but that's an illusion. The fact is, they're not failing because they're not putting themselves in situations that are testing them. They're not opening those doors. They're not bursting those bubbles. They don't understand that when you crash out every now and then it's a sign that you're smashing into new corridors, learning, growing, improving yourself, even if slowly. Those calluses and bruises and scars on your skin are not signs of failure, but success.

CHAPTER 9

DEATH IS OTHER PEOPLE

CAMP 1 WAS a grim plain of rocks and nothing. As soon as we stumbled into it I located the tent that had been set up for me, dived into it and began squaring my kit away to the extent that I needed to – for as short a stay as possible. I was eager to enjoy my final dose of solitude. This would be the last of the four camps on the mountain in which I'd have a place of my own to sleep. From now on we'd be sharing. I lit my gas burner and prepared myself a pot of Nepalese 'RaRa' ramen noodles, which I ate without much relish as the lack of oxygen had done its numbing work on my appetite. I rubbed my temples to soothe my headache. My mood was slightly flat and I felt bored. I soon realised that it wasn't only me. Nobody else in camp really wanted to talk, and most of the climbers knew to respect each other's wishes.

But not all of them. After I'd had about ten minutes' rest I left my tent for a bit of a wander and a look about. I was keen to get my blood pumping again and try to distract myself into a better head space. When I found a quiet spot I pulled my camera out, set it up and began the process of filming a little piece for broadcast. Seeing what I was up to, a tall Italian climber in a blue jacket strode confidently but unsmilingly up to me.

'When are you looking at summiting?' he asked.

The answer was, I was keen to summit the moment it was possible. I was desperate to power ahead and get up and then down again as quickly as I could in order to avoid the masses. The intelligence I'd received from Dawa told me that the fixing team weren't going to be done up on the summit until 14 April, so that was the target date I'd planted firmly in my mind.

'The 14th,' I told him.

'The 14th?' he said. He nodded, unimpressed, and placed a hand on his hip. 'We're looking at three days before that.'

Here we go. I knew exactly the kind of man I was dealing with here. If I'd told him I was summiting in my underpants he would have said he was doing it naked on his hands for the Princess of Monaco's Save the Pink Elephant fund. I was not in the mood for this. I'd just come out of eight hours in the icefall, I'd been trying to mind my own business, and here I was being challenged by Biggerbollocks in his spotless designer mountain-wear.

'OK, well, well done, mate,' I said, mirthlessly. 'Good on you. I like your style. I'll see you up there.'

We set off for Camp II a couple of days later. After the drama of the icefall, ascending the snowfields of the Western

Cwm came as a welcome change of pace. It wasn't much of a technical challenge, mostly a gradual climb up this enormously wide and spectacular amphitheatre. It was a long, steady slog, but the view of constantly shifting Himalayan peaks was more than enough to keep our morale up.

Not that it was completely without obstacles. We soon discovered that about halfway up the Cwm a massive twenty-five-metre ice step had recently opened up. There was no way around it. We had to climb. The fixing team had left a ladder in place that enabled one climber at a time to start up its face for a distance of about four metres. After that, there was a twenty-odd-metre climb up a rope that took you the rest of the way. Once you'd climbed the ladder you had to pull yourself upright so you were standing up on your legs on its highest rung. Then you had to clip your jumar onto the rope, kick your feet into the ice wall with the front points of your crampons and climb up the rope, using your jumar to safeguard your ascent. It was a little tricky, but it was mountaineering. It was what we were there to do.

When Ed, Dawa and I reached the step I was surprised to find a queue had already formed. As early as we were in the climbing season, it seemed that we still hadn't managed to avoid the logjams. And there right in front of me, look who it was – my old friend Biggerbollocks. Perfect. When it was finally his turn to climb, I stood back to watch him tackle it. He made painfully slow progress up the ladder, wobbling this way and that, fussing with his crampons, constantly looking down. I couldn't be sure whether he was shaking with the cold or with fear.

When he finally got to the top of the ladder he clipped his jumar onto the rope ... and then stopped. We watched him for a while in confused silence. He was supposed to kick his boots into the ice wall with his crampons, but he looked like he didn't quite know how to do it. He didn't have faith that they would hold in the ice, the result being that he was scared to get off the ladder. This could only really have been down to a lack of experience. The three of us stood by, with growing irritation, as he jabbed one foot into the ice wall, leaned incorrectly into it, and flopped over to one side. And then did it again. And did it again.

'This is embarrassing,' I muttered to Ed, who was busy filming it all.

After nearly an hour of hanging around, a bottleneck of between thirty and forty people had stacked up behind us. The cold had started to get to me. My team's morale was suffering. I'd had enough. I wasn't going to let this pillock ruin the days of all these people.

I walked to the base of the ice wall and shouted up, 'Right, mate, you're going to have to come down that ladder now.'

He didn't answer.

After I'd called up a couple more times, I decided to address his Sherpa team. 'Guys, you're going to have to get this guy down,' I said. 'He can't do it. There's forty people down here. We've got to get moving.'

One of his Sherpas peered down from the top of the ice wall.

'No, no, no, we're going to pull him up,' he said.

'Pull him up? What do you mean?'

'Pulley system at the top,' he said.

I was about to ask Dawa what the hell was going on when I saw a rope flop down from the top of the step. The Italian clipped onto it and his Sherpa team began pulling. And there he went, bouncing up the ice step like a baby being rescued from a well. A couple of minutes after they'd hauled him over the lip of the step I was up there behind him.

'You shouldn't be on the mountain,' I told him.

'No!' he protested.

'You can't even get up that,' I said, pointing back down the step. 'What makes you think you can get up there?'

'Ah, yeah, yeah,' he said blandly, trying to swat me away.

'It's a joke. You're paying to be hauled up the mountain. I'm shocked.'

He turned away from me.

'Are you carrying on?' I said. 'Are you actually going up there?'

He held out his hand out for me to shake.

'Good luck,' he said.

'Yeah, good luck to you as well,' I said, grabbing onto this hand. 'You're going to need it.'

It was a huge reality check. This man was a serious danger to other climbers. Forget about the avalanches, forget about the death zone, forget about the icefall, the unpredictable weather, the altitude. The real threat came from these idiots who were paying tens of thousands of dollars just to be able to tell their mates back home that they'd climbed Everest, when the truth was they'd been manhandled all the way up by Sherpas. It came from people like him, who have plenty of money to spare and have grown tired of using it to show off with nice clothes, fast cars and fancy homes, and have instead decided that they want to stand on the top of the world.

It was an ego thing. And ego gets you into trouble. I'd seen these kinds of individuals operating in war zones. Being motivated by ego, I've noticed, is the quickest way of getting yourself killed. It makes you delusional and overconfident. It makes you cut corners. Every decision you make ends up being based not on reading the situation and following the correct procedure but on how good you're going to look.

Of course, what this man was lacking was the healthy motivation of pride. Whereas ego takes the easy route, pride means you do things properly even when nobody is watching. Pride means that you're constantly looking for ways to test yourself, improve yourself and learn to do it better. But just like Chris in that little sailing boat in the Pacific Ocean, when you're motivated by ego you never think you need to test yourself because you're already convinced you've got it. You deserve that medal of the summit. It's simply a case of being dragged up there and blaming other people – or the situation – when things go wrong. If you're motivated by pride you'd never dream of wearing that medal until you were absolutely convinced you had the right to. Pride means you put yourself through whatever you need to in order to fully warrant the prize.

This is one of the lessons the military teaches you. You earn your right of passage. You can't bypass it. There's lots of talk at the moment about the fact that the Ministry of Defence has started allowing women on the Special Forces Selection course. I've got no problem with that – as long as each and every female candidate for the SAS or SBS has shown that they deserve to be there and are not just motivated by ego.

What most civilians don't understand is that it's not simply about turning up at Special Forces Selection and cracking on. It's about earning your seat there in the first place. You can apply after two years of military service, from any cap badge, but it helps to have been a paratrooper, a Marine or an elite infantry soldier, with five to seven years of an exemplary military career, including a tour of duty. And all of that achievement just gets you a place, not on Selection, but on Pre-Selection. Only once you've passed Pre-Selection have you earned your seat at the table. Anyone, man or woman, who is motivated by pride would not want to cheat that process or plead for special treatment. Sitting there with the others on day one of Selection, you need to have already proved yourself to be a truly exceptional individual. And after that? Six months of physical and psychological hell – not to mention the 95 per cent failure rate that had got my old buddy Bench so paralysed with fear.

Whether it's on Selection, in service with the Special Forces or anywhere else, dealing with fear is much easier for the person who's motivated by pride. For these people, being in incredibly fearful situations is easier because the fear itself is part of the test. But if you're motivated by ego, that fear comes as a shock. You're great, so why should you be frightened? What's that fear doing there? Amazing people like you don't feel fear. So you push it away. Just like Chris, you act in denial. In fearful situations pride is earned but ego is bruised. Whenever someone tells me that they're 'fearless', I take it as a sign that they're motivated by the wrong forces. They're delusional. And they've never truly been tested.

This is what Biggerbollocks didn't understand. If he'd had any pride in himself he would have quit there and then. When I'd confronted him he would have said, 'Yes, I'm going to hold my hands up to it. This isn't the place for me, I need to go back and train.' It shocked me when he said he was carrying on. If he'd turned back, there and then, I'd have grabbed hold of him and said, 'Good effort, mate. Train hard and give it another crack.' I like people who accept their weaknesses. I didn't like him.

As we pressed on into that epic natural arena of snow and sky, I thought about the disaster in 1996 and the number of lives that were lost, in part, because of all those people near the summit who hadn't earned the right to be there and who ended up causing problems for others that ultimately led to their deaths. I'd naïvely imagined things would have changed over the last couple of decades. In order to get above Base Camp you had to apply for an official permit that cost $11,000 per person. These permits alone raked in $4.5 million every year for the Nepalese government. If they decided to demand a basic level of climbing experience in return for one of these passes, lives would be saved every single year. So what was the reason that they didn't? I could think of four and a half million of them.

After a long, slow day trudging up the snowy gradient of the Western Cwm we finally reached Camp II. Sitting at the base of the Lhotse Face – a forbidding 1,100-metre wall of shining blue glacial ice – the camp was split into a southern and a northern zone, just over a mile apart. We found our tents right at the top end of the northern zone. The leap in altitude from Base Camp was noticeable. Here, at the upper limit of the Western Cwm, we were 6,500 metres above sea level, higher than I'd ever been before.

By now, although altitude sickness was really grinding into me, things were noticeably worse for some of the others. Walking around the camp it was obvious that a lot of the Westerners were truly suffering. Some had terrible pounding headaches, while others were huddled behind rocks coughing up phlegm and vomiting. It wasn't long before the helicopters started coming. Camp II was the last rescue point on

Everest. From now on we'd be walking into the abyss, on our own among the litter of frozen corpses. It didn't come as a great surprise to discover that my old friend Biggerbollocks was one of the climbers who'd been flown back down to Base Camp. But it was a relief. The simple fact of having him off the slopes was a supercharger for my morale.

The idea was to stay at Camp II for another day, so our bodies could get used to the altitude, and then return to Base Camp, where we'd spend another week. We'd then begin our second rotation. This meant climbing back up through the icefall, more time in Camp I, up the Western Cwm again, get to Camp II again, and then scale the Lhotse Face, touch Camp III, and make it all the way back down again. After that would be rotation three. Then, finally, we'd start at Base Camp again for the final summit rotation.

To which I thought, 'Fuck that.'

'When are we going down?' asked Ed, over steaming cups of tea following our second night in Camp II. He was lying next to me in our shared tent, propped up on his arm. 'Tonight? Or do we do another twenty-four hours here?'

'I don't know if I feel the need to,' I said.

A flash of concern came over his face. 'Yeah, we should go down and do another rotation.'

'I feel fine,' I said. 'In fact – you know what? I feel like I could touch Camp III.'

'What, Camp III? Now?' he said. 'Jesus. Camp II to III is a serious climb.'

I braced myself for a battle. Here it was, exactly what I didn't want. I had to keep reminding myself that this was my expedition. Ed was here to film me. He was following me up, not calling the shots. Clearly he was about to dig his heels in, but there was no way I was going to let him. I was climbing to Camp III whether he was coming with me or not. If that meant a row, it meant a row. The problem was, he didn't understand my level of resilience. He didn't know what I was capable of. He hadn't grasped why I was really here. I wanted to test myself. I wanted 'serious'. I wanted that trouble. I wanted fear.

'Mate, I feel fine,' I said, before batting it back for him. 'Why, how do you feel?'

There was silence. And then, to my surprise and relief, a broad smile unleashed itself across Ed's face.

'Fuck it. Let's do it.'

THE CLIMB BETWEEN Camp II and Camp III, up the Lhotse Face and beyond, is tough at the best of times. If you slip off the rope on the face you're dead. It's this knife edge between living and dying that gets inside people's heads and turns them towards the negative. It doesn't take an athlete-standard level of fitness to reach Camp III, but your mindset has to be spot on. I saw people on the mountain who were incredibly fit physically and coping perfectly well with the altitude, but who ended up getting helicoptered out of there. The mountain had become one enormous fear bubble for them. They were in it for too long. It drained them. It defeated them.

As difficult as it was, this climb would be tougher for us than for most others. Not only were we tired and lacking the physical and psychological benefits of a second rotation, we were tackling the climb so early in the season that there was no well-trodden route up through the ice and snow – no worn steps to put your foot in after having climbed up for five hundred feet, no clear track over the hidden crevasses and past the daunting obstacles. But it was worth it. I was determined to break away from the pack as much as we possibly could. And I wanted to test myself. So we pushed on upwards into the deadly folds of the mountain, and had soon climbed so high that we could actually see the fixing team, working hundreds of metres above us, scoping out and securing this season's route to the top.

When we finally hit Camp III it was almost deserted. There were only a couple of tents set up there in that breathless, sun-blind expanse of snow, and they were for the fixing team. As exhausted as we were, I felt an enormous sense of achievement. For the first time since the beginning of this adventure, we'd proved ourselves to be better than the average Everest tourist. We were beginning to excel. We'd climbed to 7,200 metres with no rotations necessary. It felt incredible. As I embraced Ed and we slapped each other's backs, I also realised that something seemed to have switched in him. Things were easier between us. That unspoken, jostling tension that had kept crackling had vanished. I sensed that my making the decision not to go back to Base Camp but to push on upwards had finally convinced him that I was worthy of a place on the mountain. Now, I hoped, he would start to fully trust me.

I didn't want to leave straight away, as the longer your body spends in Camp III getting used to the lack of oxygen, the more benefit you ultimately gain. We prepared another small meal of ramen noodles on a portable stove and ate them slightly joylessly. I was mindful that, beyond here, eating would only become harder. Any higher and we'd be lucky to get anything solid down us at all – we'd probably only be sipping soup. Beyond Camp IV, the human digestive system stops working completely.

With Camp III taken care of, we began the long return journey back to Base Camp. By the time we hit Camp II my appetite had come roaring back. I took full advantage of the availability of Sherpa cooks, and stuffed down as much meat and potatoes as I could handle. After a night there, the three of us negotiated the Khumbu Icefall with its endless ladders and ropes, and the next thing I knew I was squaring my kit away back at Base Camp, which was now buzzing with climbers and trekkers.

'Is the first day we can hit the summit still 14 April?' I asked Dawa later that afternoon.

'I'll check,' he said. 'I think that's still the first window after the fixing team have finished.'

'Can we follow the fixing team up?' I asked.

Dawa being Dawa, he didn't like to say no, but I could tell by his expression that this wouldn't be considered appropriate.

'OK,' I said. 'Let's not put too much pressure on them. But as soon as it's fixed, we need to be in a position to go the next day. I want to be first man in, up on the summit.'

'We will try,' he said. 'When are we going to leave for our second rotation?'

'I'll let you know,' I said. 'Soon. We'll do it soon.'

But would we? Did I definitely need to complete another rotation? Could I get away with not doing one? Or would that mean I'd be putting myself at undue risk? That night, over yet more meat and potatoes, I fell into conversation with a Western guide called Conan. He told me he'd been part of the fixing team as high as Camp III. He'd just arrived back from setting up the ropes up there, and I could tell he was an extremely strong individual.

'Do I need another rotation?' I asked him.

'Yeah, it would be a good idea,' he said. 'A second rotation's only going to help you out. You're just going to get stronger.'

'I know it's a good idea,' I said. 'But do I need one?'

He thought for a moment. 'You're as strong as an ox, mate. I reckon you'll be OK.'

That was all I needed to hear. I paced down to the large tent in which the transports were organised and popped my head through the door. Most of the workers were Sherpas, and there was a professional, slightly harassed atmosphere to the place, with its folders and phones and walkie-talkies and a well-worn computer keyboard.

'Is it possible get a helicopter down to Namche Bazaar, guys?' I asked one of them who was sitting with a half-drunk coffee at a foldaway table. Namche Bazaar is the capital of the Nepalese Sherpa. There were hotels there. Proper beds. And oxygen. Lots of delicious oxygen.

'That, uh … can be done,' he said.

'Excellent,' I said. 'How soon?'

'Earliest is tomorrow morning, if the weather holds.'

'Amazing, mate. And how much does it cost.'

'Namche Bazaar? Two thousand US per person. Payment up front.'

'Do you accept Visa Debit?'

I caught up with Ed the following morning at breakfast. 'I'm ready for the summit rotation,' I told him. 'I don't need to go up again.'

He frowned at me over his coffee. 'Are you sure?'

'100 per cent,' I said.

'Straight up to the summit?'

'Straight up, mate.'

There was a silence.

'You know, you really should do a second rotation.'

'A second rotation? Where to?' I said.

He looked exasperated. 'To Camp III!'

'But I did that in my first rotation,' I said irritably. 'What's the point in doing it again?'

Ed was the kind of man who liked to stick to the path. He didn't gel with my 'Fuck this' attitude. I could respect that well enough. What worked for him obviously worked for him and, to be fair, had got him up to that summit three times. But Ed wasn't me.

'The summit's not going to be open for another week,' he said. 'You're much better off using that time to do another rotation. Otherwise we're going to be hanging around here for bloody days. It's not getting any quieter with all these trekkers and climbers pouring in. It doesn't make any sense not to do another rotation. I say we get on out there again. Come on, mate. It's crazy just to stick around here.'

I put my mug down and stood up to leave. 'I'm out of here, Ed. It's all organised. I'm going to Namche Bazaar for a bit.'

'You're going to Namche?' He looked slightly hurt. 'Oh, right. So you've booked yourself a helicopter?'

'I've only got about half an hour to get it, so I'd better …'

'OK. Right. OK. Well, rest up when you get there, mate,' he said. 'Top up your oxygen. Use the time wisely, won't you?'

'Yeah, yeah, yeah. I'll see you when I get back.'

* * *

AFTER TOUCHING DOWN at Namche, the sense of elation I felt the moment I ducked out of the helicopter was enormous. For the first time in getting on for a month there were no cameras pointing at me, no schedule bearing down on me and no alpha-male politics to negotiate. I was free. Not only that, I'd booked myself into the best hotel in town. The Yeti Mountain Home had a fully appointed restaurant and king-size beds with electric blankets, and was located on the upper slopes of the town, which was scattered around an elbow-shaped crook of mountain ridge 3,340 metres above sea level.

The plan was to get there as soon as possible, have a hot shower, fill my belly, get my digestive system back up and running, and generally take proper care of myself for the next four days. It was imperative that I used the time to recover and then come back stronger than ever. Mounting a summit bid after having only completed one rotation was highly unusual, especially for someone as inexperienced at high altitudes as I was. I'd taken a massive risk, insisting to Ed and Dawa that I could do it. Perhaps I'd slipped and allowed ego to drive my behaviour. If that was the case, the only sensible thing I could do was admit it and use this opportunity wisely. I couldn't allow myself to fail now.

I was trotting up a flight of stone steps on my way to the hotel, when I passed a small, white, clapboard-covered building. It was decorated with the flags of the world and had a green neon sign above its grubby white door: The Irish

Pub. I found myself pausing in front of it. I looked at it. The Irish Pub. Well, I never. Yes, indeed. 'Keep walking, Ant,' I thought.

But, somehow, I didn't keep walking. Instead, I had a tense conversation with myself.

'I'll just stop for one pint.'

'No, you won't. If you stop for one pint you'll be in there all day.'

'I can handle it. One pint. Just a nice quickie cold one. Then I'll check into the hotel and rest up.'

'Bullshit.'

'One pint.'

'No such thing.'

'One pint.'

'Go to bed.'

'One pint.'

'Fuck it.'

'Top man.'

'Cheers.'

On the other side of the wooden door was a dingy space – a couple of pool tables, a dart board, ratty armchairs and sofas, and a long bar with shelves of spirits behind it. A sign above a mangy old stuffed yak's head said, 'Do not drop cigarette ends on the floor, as they burn the hands and knees of customers as they leave'. Because it was still mid-morning, the only person in there was the owner, who nodded at me in greeting from the far side of the bar. I took my place on one of the rickety stools and had a look at the offerings on the drinks menu: Khumbu Icefall, Sex on Mountain, Donkey Piss, Sherpa Killer, Yeti Fuck.

'I'll just have a beer, please, mate,' I said.

'What kind of beer would you like, sir? What do you fancy?'

'Whatever the local type is.'

'Himalayan Red?'

'That's the one.'

He pulled a clean glass from under the counter and began filling it with a can from the fridge.

'You don't look much like a trekker,' he said, as he poured.

'No, I'm a climber,' I told him. 'Just got down from Camp III.'

'You've been to Camp III already? Woah!'

We soon fell into talking. The barman told me his name was Krishna, I told him about my wife and children, and then he told me about his. Eight pints later I realised I'd found a brand new best friend. The only problem was, this was exactly the wrong time and place to find a new best friend.

Over the next few days I ended up basically living in Krishna's bar. I'd stumble out, smashed, at 2 a.m. every night. Then I'd wake up feeling dreadful, with the symptoms of my hangover concentrated dozens of times over by the effects of high altitude, cram a bit of lunch down my throat and then be back in to see Krishna until the early hours. On my fourth and final day in Namche I swore to myself that I'd be sensible. I wouldn't go and see Krishna. I'd lie in, eat healthily and heartily, and maybe take advantage of the luxury spa in the hotel. I departed from Krishna's bar that night at 3 a.m. A few hours later, as the helicopter lifted off for the short journey back to Base Camp, I couldn't wait to get away from my new best friend.

I located Ed and Dawa in the Madison Mountaineering area. They were sitting on camp chairs chatting when I strode up confidently towards them, hoping the wind would blow away the alcohol fumes that were billowing off me like the plumes of snow that continually tail off Everest's black summit.

'Did you rest well?' asked Dawa.

'Really well,' I said. 'Feel great.' I looked over my shoulder so I could let free a long, poisonous burp. 'Yes, mate. Can't wait to crack on.'

The truth was, I felt like rotting meat. But, I told myself, I'd done the damage and now I had to live with the consequences. I'd just have to push through. I'd be devastated if I didn't end up making the summit because I'd been out on the lash. If I didn't get up there, for whatever reason, I knew I'd end up blaming it on Namche Bazaar. I had to take responsibility for what I'd done. I'd messed up. The only thing I could do was to turn it into a positive. Now I had one more reason why I couldn't allow myself to fail.

'Hey, Ant, I've been thinking,' said Ed. 'Have you considered doing the summit without oxygen?'

'What do you mean?' I asked.

I couldn't quite process what he was saying. Without oxygen? Ever since the first British attempt on the mountain in 1922, climbing high on the mountain with the aid of supplementary oxygen tanks has been fairly standard, although three British climbers had reached 28,126 feet without it on the unsuccessful 1933 expedition. Even the Sherpas, with their fabled 'superhuman' powers, use it. The idea of attempting this feat without oxygen hadn't even occurred to me. The death zone is called the death zone for a reason. And that reason is death.

'Is that even possible?' I asked.

He shrugged. 'It's possible. It's been done. You should think about it.'

'I will,' I said. 'Yes, I will.'

CHAPTER 10

THE FEAR OF CONFLICT

ONE OF THE greatest human fears of all is the fear of upsetting other people. So many people spend their entire lives engaged in the utterly hopeless mission of trying to get everyone they meet to like them. Unlike guys like Bench, Chris and Biggerbollocks, who wrap their entire identity around success and achievement, these men and women base their sense of self-esteem around popularity. They fear conflict because they cannot cope with the idea that someone might not want to be their pal. But the fear of conflict can be just as debilitating as the fear of suffering or failure. It's another major source of sticky boots. It roots people to the spot, preventing them from stepping into their fear bubbles and opening doors of opportunity. Like all varieties of fear, if you fail to harness it, it will shrink you.

HOW TO INOCULATE YOURSELF AGAINST CRITICISM

But before we get into popularity, let's have a close look at another issue that comes up when we think about conflict. We're not only scared that if we stand up to a person they'll decide not to like us. We're also afraid that in the heat of the argument we'll learn something negative about ourselves. We're worried that if we take an opponent on we'll be confronted, not with another person, but with a mirror showing us a horrible reflection of who we really are – a reflection that will just be too upsetting to deal with. This is simply human nature. No one likes to hear bad things about themselves.

But there is a surprisingly easy way of dampening down this fear of criticism. The fact is, the only way such a fear can ever become real – and someone can actually tell us something that knocks us to our knees – is if we've allowed ourselves to become deluded about who we are in the first place. I know this because it's exactly what happened to me when I was a young lad. As a teenager I used to strut around with my little pigeon chest out thinking I was the mutt's nuts. I left home to join the army, became a member of the Royal Engineers, completed my parachute course and ended up in 9 Parachute Squadron. And I did well. I was named the best at physical training and best overall recruit.

But nearly five years after joining the army I made the decision to leave. I'd slowly become isolated from the other men in my squadron and I wasn't enjoying it any more. Partly this was due to the fact that I had a wife and young son, and this regularly took me away from the lads. It was also partly because their typical squaddie lifestyle of heavy drinking and bad behaviour had come to seem increasingly dull to me, and the other guys in the squad correctly took my lack of enthusiasm for joining in with it all as a sign of disrespect. But there was also a third reason for my increasing isolation. People were saying I'd become cocky. Puffed up. Not a team player. That was bullshit, as far as I was concerned. I was sure they were wrong. It wasn't my cockiness that was putting their noses out of joint, it was the fact that I thought their idea of fun – throwing darts into each other's backs, dangling their bollocks into the pockets of the pub pool tables and having pool balls smashed into them – was ridiculous, embarrassing and boring.

When I finally left the military I didn't feel at all worried. With experience and ability like mine, I had zero doubt that I'd smash it in civvy street. So off I went, out into the real world and through the doors of my local job centre. I'd come armed with a red book that everyone gets when they leave the military containing their credentials, qualifications and a final report. As I trotted up the steps and through the doors, the man behind the job centre counter clocked my book immediately. I smiled to myself. This was pretty exciting. Who knew where my new life would take me? As I pulled the chair out and sat down, I knew how our conversation would go. I'd been rehearsing it in my head for weeks: 'I'm looking for a top private security job, maybe as a celebrity bodyguard or, seeing as I speak fluent French, as an interpreter at the United Nations or Interpol or MI6, if they're looking.'

The man behind the desk flicked through my book with obvious interest. I waited in silence for a few moments.

'So why did you leave the army?' he said.

'Just wanted to make it in the real world.' I shrugged.

He passed the book back to me. 'Well, I can tell you this. I've seen hundreds of these little books and this is one of the best that's ever come across my desk.'

'Ha ha, top man,' I said. 'That's what I like to hear.' I sat back in my seat, grinned widely and nodded. 'So what do you think you can get me then?'

'Well, I can definitely get you a job as a bin man.'

Ten minutes later I was sitting on the steps outside the job centre with my head in my hands. On the step beneath me was a man with two teeth in his skull and no laces in his shoes. He was visibly rattling. I had a silent word with myself. 'How did this happen? How did you get to be on the steps of Chelmsford Job Centre sitting next to bloody Nobby Two Teeth here?' The only way I could answer that question in any useful way was by being brutally honest with myself. For the first time in my life I ripped myself to shreds. I was absolutely merciless. 'You think you're better than everyone else. You're not a team player. You've isolated yourself. No one wants to be around you. Your confidence has tipped so far over into ego that you've lost who you are. It's fucking ego that's done this to you. You can't carry on like this. You've got to get a hold of yourself. You've got to rein it in.'

That moment was painful, but it freed me. Now I'd told myself some bitter home truths, I knew exactly what I had to work on and, moreover, had inoculated myself against criticism that had once stung badly. No one could use any of it against me any more. From that day on when people said, 'Ant, you're a bit big-headed,' I'd simply reply, 'Yep, I know that. And I'm working on it. Thanks very much.' And, the truth is, I'm still working on it. Even today, whenever I get a bit carried away with myself, I always take myself back to that moment on the steps. Everyone has their particular flaws that they're going to struggle with, in one way or another, for the rest of their lives. That's fine. It's this struggle that makes us all better people. It's this struggle that takes courage. It's this struggle that makes us grow. Everyone's struggle is different. I know that this is mine – and that means I never deny it. I know my whole person. So when people sling any accurate criticism at me, it never really hurts.

BRUTAL HONESTY PREVENTS CRITICAL ERRORS

This brutal honesty I practise with myself also means that I'm better able to spot it when a flaw of character is leading someone into errors of judgement. Whenever we allow ourselves to remain deluded about the parts of us that aren't perfect, we become susceptible to making serious mistakes. One example of this was contestant number fourteen from Series 3 of *SAS: Who Dares Wins*. The events around this young man's withdrawal from the show made for probably the most controversial scenes in the programme's history to date. And I can totally understand why. What everyone saw on the TV was an exhausted contestant who was simply refusing to give up – and yet, there I was, shouting at him, 'Give me your fucking armband, you're off!' So why was I punishing this apparently perfect vision of soldierly grit and determination with such ferocity? Because the man was deluding himself, and his delusions were damaging the rest of his team.

It was towards the end of the show and the contestants were already reaching the limits of their mental and physical abilities. Late in the afternoon, after a long, tough day, we instructed them to do a round robin out on the mountainside. It involved running on a diamond-shaped track of about 300 metres and carrying heavy boulders, with the contestants knowing that we intended to keep it going until at least one of them quit. It became rapidly apparent that contestant number fourteen was in far worse shape than the rest as he was dragging far behind everyone else. Soon he was fully two and a half minutes away from the next man. There was no way that he was ever going to catch up.

'You're going to get binned after this,' I told him. 'But you can stop your teammates from suffering right now by handing in your armband. If you do that, I'll stop the exercise.'

He refused.

People started lapping him. Then they lapped him twice over. Still he refused to accept the inevitable, put the team out of their misery and quit. What especially annoyed me was that, because he didn't hand his armband in, someone else lost their spirit and left the process. And this other contestant was doing really well. I felt absolutely gutted for him. So I went back to number fourteen.

'People are suffering now,' I told him. 'And you're going home after this. So give me your fucking armband.'

But he kept on refusing. In a further attempt to drive my point home, I stopped the rest of his team, put them in agonising stress positions on the rocky ground and made him watch them.

'You can stop them suffering for a further couple of hours if you hand me your number,' I said.

He continued to refuse. The men started crying out in pain and beseeching him: 'Come on, do the right thing, man,' and 'Fucking give it up, mate.'

I asked him one more time. 'Listen to your men. Listen to your team. And do the right thing.'

But yet again he refused.

So I ripped his armband off and sent him home.

Following the broadcast of these scenes I received a flood of criticism on social media. Then, when Channel 4 posted it all on YouTube, over a thousand mostly critical commenters piled in: 'Ant blew up because the bloke had more patience than him. Pathetic display'; 'This "trainer" is a jerk. The goal is not to kick the weakest guy off. The goal is to keep going and that's what the weaker guy did. He didn't give up'; 'Lost a lot of respect for Ant here'; 'Can't stand the guy in the black who thinks he's better than anyone.'

They simply didn't get it. The problem was that number fourteen was utterly deluded about himself. He'd fallen so far behind the others that he could never recover. Anyone could see that. He should have been able to see that. But his absolute inability to be honest about himself was seriously damaging his teammates. He had already failed badly both on physical fitness and on teamwork, and was simply carrying on for the sake of his ego, where a man of pride would have done the dignified thing and stopped. In the battlefield this contestant would have been a massive liability to his men. There was no question he had to go. Yes, he was showing guts and determination. But what sort of message are we sending if we say if you've got guts and determination you'll always succeed? That's not reality.

And all those people criticising me on the internet? They can't really affect me. I'm not afraid of what they have to say because I already know what's wrong about me and I already know what's right about me. My own honesty makes me pretty much bulletproof from these kinds of comments. And this, in turn, helps to prevent me cowering away from interpersonal conflict. I'm not worried about standing up for myself and initiating it, because I know that nothing my opponent will say can be worse than anything I've said to myself.

I don't believe it's possible to maintain a positive mindset if you can't be brutally honest with yourself. Without such honesty you can't hold yourself accountable for your actions. Brutal honesty frees you as an individual. No one can tell you who you are, because you know yourself better than anyone else. People will always want to talk about your negative points and they'll rarely talk about your successes. They're writing a story about who you are with only a fraction of the necessary information. Even your wife and parents only know a slice of you. Only you know what you're really like. Only you know if you have sadistic thoughts or if you're a bit of an animal. Only you know if and when you've failed. The crucial thing is to not deny those failures. The moment you put up walls around your flaws, you're hiding them from yourself and that prevents you from growing. And if you do that, you'll never find out what you're truly capable of.

BRUTAL HONESTY FOR YOU, RESPECTFUL HONESTY FOR OTHERS

Just as you should practise brutal honesty with yourself, you should also be honest with others. This is not to say that you should be outwardly disrespectful, of course, but it does mean you should strive to have the courage to make plain-spoken truth a higher priority than your own popularity. You can't expect to succeed in life if you're scared to tell people what you really think. Humans have evolved to operate in teams. That's how we survive. That's how we progress. And what keeps human teams functional is honest communication. When people become Yes men or women, they're acting out of fear. It's a sign that they're stuck in their corridors. They're not leaders, they're followers. They're never going to be any use to the team because they're not contributing their honest point of view. If you look very closely at the average Yes man, I swear you can almost see him physically shrinking before your eyes.

This is partly why I'm so critical of the extreme politically correct turn that society seems to have taken over the last few years. We succeed, as a species, when we feel free to speak honestly, respectfully and directly to each other. Everyone's beliefs are different. What's worked for me, and my experience, is different from what's worked for you, and your experience. That's how it should be. Different kinds of people get together, share their different beliefs and experiences, debate them, take what's best and discard the rest – and then progress. But everyone gets told what to say and think these days. They're not allowed to honestly share their views. They're being pressured to lie about their beliefs. I refuse to comply with this politically correct culture. When you take honesty out of a situation and allow one group to force their views on another, negative things follow.

DON'T TAKE IT PERSONALLY

If you're ever going to maximise your potential, you need to be able to acknowledge 100 per cent of yourself, not 50. Only then will you know what you're fully capable of and be able to live without limits. Sometimes your attempts at being brutally honest with yourself will come up short and you'll find yourself in a situation in which you have to learn the harsh lesson that other people have got to tell you. That takes courage, but it's something positive and is totally worth it. It's just crucial that you don't take such criticism personally.

I know it's not easy. But even when I was in the Special Forces and people were firing at me, I never took it personally. If I'd done so, I'd have put myself at risk of losing control. Some of the best advice I received came from an officer I served under in the SBS.

'Ant,' he said, 'what's your job as an SBS point man? What would you say were your principal objectives?'

'To look after my team, look after myself and kill the bad guys,' I said.

'You've got two out of three. You don't go out there to kill the bad guys. Your primary job is to save life, not take it. If you don't have to take that shot, then don't.'

Today it's those moments in the battlefield that I actually remember most – the times I took my finger off the trigger because I didn't need to take the shot. If I'd taken war personally, I wouldn't have been able to do that. I had to acknowledge I was in a brutal world and that some of my pals might not come back. But *I* had put myself in that situation, just as my pals had. These bullets that were firing at us were *our* responsibility. *We* had placed ourselves in the line of fire. It was no good blaming other people. Even when enemy combatants were firing directly at me, they weren't thinking, 'Oh, it's Ant Middleton. Let's kill him.' It was never personal. It was just war.

But even I have to pull myself up every now and then. Not long ago there were plans to make a limited edition Action Man of me, the proceeds of which would go to the Royal National Lifeboat Institution. I'd spent some time working with the team, the design had been finalised and it was about to go into manufacture. The day before it did, and I was to announce the Action Man at a big press conference, the entire project was cancelled. It turned out that someone was offended that I'd served a prison sentence and had contacted the manufacturers to complain. To be completely honest, I did take it personally at first. 'Wow, someone's obviously out to get me,' I thought. 'They've got a personal vendetta against me. I've not hidden my past. It's not a secret. Anyone can see that's not who I am any more.' But I had to shake it off. Someone out there had obviously let negativity get hold of them and I wasn't going to take it on board. The negativity was theirs, not mine.

As a former member of the military, I'm well aware how damaging it can be to someone's mindset if they take everything personally. These days I spend a lot of time talking to people who are struggling with the psychological issues that are sadly all too typical in those who've experienced the horrors of war. Just three days ago I spoke to a serving Royal Marine who told me he wanted to commit suicide.

'You think so positively and I think so negatively,' he said.

'I cannot fathom what you're thinking right now,' I told him. 'But you've clearly got a powerful mind. An amazing mind. You will get to where I am because you've lain in the pits of hell and you're pushing your way through it. That extreme way of thinking can be flipped.'

He told me he believed his negative mindset had its roots in his experience of war. He'd seen his friend get blown up by an IED in Afghanistan. As we talked, it became apparent to me that he'd taken it personally. He'd become stuck in a cycle of thinking, 'Why is he dead? I should be dead. I'm going to kill myself to make it fair.' But the people who laid that IED didn't say, 'Right, that's going to be your mate. We're going to make sure he gets blown up in front of you.' The brain always wants to create this negative chatter. It pounces on any evidence of danger in the world that it sees and uses it in a way that's supposed to protect you. In cases like this man's, the process had gone haywire. His mind played on the events of war, dwelling obsessively on the horror, constantly returning to it in an attempt to prevent him from ever going into such a situation again.

I told that Marine that he needed to be brutally honest about what had happened. What was the situation? And what wasn't it? He needed to acknowledge it and process it. As part of that processing, he needed to completely understand that it was not personal. Only then would he be able to move on.

EGO NEEDS PRAISE

We all know people whose main motivation in life seems to be being as popular as possible. This is a cast-iron sign that they're motivated by ego rather than healthy pride. Individuals who live or die psychologically by what other people think of them are doomed to be forever stuck in their corridors. To be ambitious you've got to be capable of enduring periods of conflict with other people, and that means they'll sometimes turn against you. You can't centre your whole life on the pursuit of pleasing other people. But that's what ego needs to do to satisfy itself. Ego needs praise. It cares too much about other people's opinions. But you can't control what other people think of you, and neither should you want to. What they think of you is up to them. Leave it to them. Pride, meanwhile, requires no external praise, and that's why it doesn't hold you back. Once you stop trying to please everyone else all the time, you become free.

THE AWESOME POWER OF ENEMIES

During the filming of Series 4 of *SAS: Who Dares Wins*, I met a man in his mid-thirties who had an amazing story to tell about how to harness the negativity of your enemies and use its power for your own ends. It was during the boxing-match phase, when we want to see how well the contestants manage conflict, and this one guy just let rip. There was a huge amount of controlled aggression inside him that we weren't expecting to see. Curious about its origins, we brought him in for a chat. He told us that he'd been badly bullied at his secondary school. He'd endure daily kickings and had his clothes stolen from the changing rooms during

PE. They'd been pissed on, and he had to walk around all day wet and stinking of urine.

When the bullying started he had three years left at school. He decided to cut himself off so much from the bullies that he'd never encounter them again. His way of ensuring this was by becoming extremely successful, thinking, 'I'm either going to let this fuck up my whole future or get my head down, get my homework done, get my exams passed, and when it does end I'll be the one who's won.' He spent those three years working incredibly hard. He ended up becoming a lawyer at a highly respected firm, while the rest of them became jobless bums. I've no doubt that all the aggression that they'd directed towards him helped make him an incredible success. That's the power of a positive mindset. He'd flipped a massive negative into massive personal success. Even in the face of such merciless bullying, he didn't take on the mindset of a victim. He assumed responsibility for his life and his situation, and this made him a better man than he would have been if his clothes had never been pissed on.

Luckily, most people won't have to endure three years of such hell. But if you step into a conflict with someone else and you happen to make a new enemy, then so what? You should always turn your enemies into energy. Use them to push you on into those new corridors. Use them to motivate you to step into your fear bubbles. Having enemies is a sign that you're progressing in life. They're a badge of honour.

There's no way of smashing through those doors of opportunity without putting a few noses out of joint. When you use the fear bubble technique, people will compete with you and lose. People will become jealous. People will talk shit about you. People will try to hold you back. Show me a person without enemies and I'll show you a person whose boots are soaked in glue – a shrinking violet, a victim, a failing person, paralysed by fear.

CHAPTER 11

CONQUERING THE KING OF THE ROCKS

THERE WAS NO doubt about it, Ed's suggestion was compelling. Even the most famous Sherpa of all, Tenzing Norgay, had reached Mount Everest's summit in 1953 with the help of an oxygen tank on his back. Sure, many highly experienced mountaineers had managed to climb Everest without oxygen, but the idea of me doing so as well – reaching the highest point on earth having never bagged a high-altitude peak before, after just one rotation and off the back of a pre-expedition diet of chicken wings and a four-day piss-up in Namche Bazaar – now that really would be something.

Over the next couple of days at Base Camp I tossed the idea around in my head. It wasn't as if there was much else to think about. The weather had turned and conditions up on the higher slopes were apparently too dangerous for us to even contemplate making an attempt on the summit. I made sure I got into the habit of waking up early and drinking tea with the kitchen staff rather than hanging out in the communal tent. That way I could find out what was really going on. I discovered that the fixing team still hadn't made it to the top because of the brutality of the weather. They were already two days late, having only got as far as a small step known as the Balcony, which sits halfway between Camp IV and the summit.

But the longer we left it, the more anxious and itchy I became. With every hour that passed it seemed as if the backlog of climbers in Base Camp was growing larger. There were now dozens and dozens of Biggerbollocks's strutting about in their spanking-new North Face down jackets, and I was desperate that we should push ahead of as many of them as possible.

That night I called a little heads-together with Ed and Dawa outside our tents.

'If we're going to get shot of this lot, we need to stick right on the heels of the fixing team,' I told them. 'I think our immediate objective should be to get to Camp II as soon as possible. Once we're there, we'll be in prime position to mount our bid on the summit. We'll take it the moment they're finished.'

'And have you thought any more about doing it without oxygen?' asked Ed.

'Yeah, yeah, I'm thinking about it,' I told him. 'But for now we just need to focus on getting up there as quickly as possible. What do you think? Stick on the heels of the fixing team?'

'Well, I don't have a massive problem with it in principle,' said Ed. 'But we can't leave here for a while. During the next couple of days, at least, the weather's supposed to be too bad.'

'I'm thinking we fight through it.'

'Fight through it?' he said. He paused to take it in. 'I honestly believe we should wait. The conditions up there ...'

'I'm sick of waiting. If we leave now, nobody will be following us. What do you think, Dawa?'

Dawa looked down at the icy ground, uncharacteristically pensive.

'To get to Camp IV, and so position ourselves correctly for the first available window, we will have to go through adverse conditions for sure,' he said.

'What does that mean exactly?' I asked. 'Adverse conditions? How adverse is adverse?'

'Reports say that bigger storms are coming over tomorrow,' he said. 'Electrical storms. Very high winds.'

'Fuck it,' I said. 'We're going to go tomorrow. Dawa, are you happy?'

'Yes.'

'Ed, are you happy?'

'Yeah.'

They weren't happy. That was as obvious as the freezing wind that was smacking against our faces. But I was determined to push on past the crowds. This was my mission and I was willing to take on the responsibility for it. This was on me.

The next morning at just after 1 a.m. we gathered in the blustery darkness around the Sherpa shrine to take part in another puja. The last time we did this ceremony the atmosphere had been one of nervous excitement. This time it was just nerves. A quiet, sombre mood had come over Ed and Dawa, and where the ritual had previously seemed exotic and alluring, all the chanting and smoke and staring stone gods now felt eerie and portentous.

Throughout the hour-long hike to the point where we donned crampons at the base of the Khumbu Icefall, nobody spoke. Shortly after we got there, it came. BA-BOOM. The sky flashed and blasted above. Strobes of white and pink light flickered across the endless canyons of ice around us, just as Dawa had promised.

'It's pretty bad,' said Ed.

'Yep,' I said.

'It's quite close,' he said.

'It's lighting up the sky,' I said. 'What do you think, Dawa? It's not a big problem, is it?'

Dawa appeared lost in thought for a quiet moment and glanced at the floor.

'I think it's not a big problem.'

'There's not a big storm right on top of us then?' Ed said in disbelief.

'Um ... erm ... not on the top,' he said. 'But below 6,000 metres I think it's fine.'

I tried to buoy them both by showing them how excited

I was. 'Boom! Boom!' I laughed. 'This is exciting shit, man!'

And it was. At least for me. *This* was why I'd come to Everest. I was getting closer to that edge – I could smell it. I felt alive. I felt free. But my enthusiasm didn't seem to be proving infectious. Their morale didn't improve. And just as the violence of the storm whipped itself into new furies and heavier snow began coming down, now settling on the brims of our hoods and shoulders of our jackets, we saw a stream of little dots of light picking their way out of the icefall. From the darkness in front of us we watched a line of climbers slowly emerge. They were Sherpas.

Ed asked to interview them. 'You're coming down again, are you?' he asked.

'Yeah, yeah,' said the man at the head of the line.

'Because of the weather?'

'It's too bad,' he said. 'I am mountain guide and I think I'm going down. It's my decision.'

That was the last thing I needed. I desperately tried to keep the mood light. 'Let's just push on,' I said cheerily. 'A bit of snow never stopped me. Happy, Ed?'

'I don't know what this means, really,' he replied.

A great flicker of mauve light illuminated the entire landscape around us. It was as if the earth itself was short-circuiting.

'Don't think about it too much, mate,' I said. 'Just get your head down, crack on.'

Then, just as I turned away from him, the sky let out its most intimidating bellow yet.

The coming hours, deep inside the icefall, saw me battling with the mountain and battling with myself. With every ice wall we climbed and every crevasse we crossed, the weather became worse and worse. And the storms in my head matched it for power. Had I made the right decision? What if things became too bad to continue? Ed had begun to lose the feeling in his fingers. What if he ended up permanently injured? What if the thunder triggered an avalanche? At times the noise became so loud that we were unsure, for a few long, agonising moments, whether it was actually thunder – or ten thousand tonnes of snow coming for us out of the blind, black void. I couldn't remember ever struggling so hard to keep my mindset positive.

Finally came the dawn. With the sky turning purple then pale blue above us, the breaking light brought some psychological relief. By the time we arrived in Camp I, the electrical storm had passed but the winds were becoming fiercely strong. We stopped there for an hour, huddled together in a two-man tent, and sipped on vegetable soup. I didn't want to eat a proper meal as that would mean unloading everything, and then we'd be running the risk of getting into the comfort zone and not wanting to continue. We were cold, tired and aching – and it was important to stay that way. I just had to try to stop morale from bottoming out.

'Let's not get demoralised,' I told them. 'We'll have a proper meal at the end of the day.' Camp II, I reminded them, had a comfortable communal tent and proper kitchen with excellent Sherpa cooks. 'We'll have a nice fat plate of curry and potatoes.'

'There's still nine hours until we get to Camp II,' said Ed, in between taking little sparrow sips of his soup.

'Hopefully we've done enough to beat the crowds,' I said. 'There's no way they're following us through that lot.'

'Aye, it was a wee bit rough,' Ed said with a smile.

'At least the icefall is done,' I said. 'It's just grind from now on.'

Nobody spoke at all as we trudged up the Western Cwm. But even if we had been in the mood for a chat, there would have been little point in trying. The winds were so strong by now that they were whipping the snow up, the conditions sometimes tipping into pure whiteout. More than once I had to warn the guys to stop walking. We literally couldn't see where we were going. The chances of simply stepping off an ice wall or falling down a crevasse were real and present. On top of the weather, fatigue was also becoming a problem, with every single footstep an effort. Even the beauty of the mountain had lost its allure. What was once breathtakingly dramatic seemed drab and unchanging, just a snowy valley with snowy walls and snowy floor. And in the sky above us? Snow. Snow. More bloody snow. The only upside was that there did seem to be hardly anyone else on the mountain. Nobody else was as crazy as we were.

The forecasts reckoned that the weather should have levelled out by the time we reached Camp II. Sure enough, sixteen hours after leaving Base Camp, as we trudged our way half-broken into camp in the late afternoon, the wind finally began dying away. We could hardly believe the sight that awaited us. Camp II had been utterly battered by the storm. Many of the tents had simply been destroyed, while others were just flapping about in the wind, reduced to little more than rags.

'This is a reality check,' I said.

'If it's like this at Camp II, can you imagine what it's like at up III and IV?' said Ed.

'And what's it like on the summit?' I replied.

It was a reassuring feeling to find our tent undamaged, crawl into it, then zip the door up tight. Every particle inside me was crying out for some proper rest, but I didn't want to go to sleep this early because then I'd get up too early. Instead I sorted all my kit out, and just generally tried to get organised and kill some time. Early in the evening the three of us gathered back together in a larger communal tent that was warmed through with gas heaters. We sat beneath the flames and began the slow process of properly thawing out. None of us were feeling especially hungry but we forced down a chicken curry, knowing that this might be the last proper meal we'd eat before we summited. The weather forecast for the next day was bad. Did I risk getting the guys to push on first thing in the morning, knowing that it would pretty much be just us up there? Or should we rest in warmth and safety until conditions improved, giving the crowds a chance to catch up?

All that was playing in the back of my mind as I chatted with Ed and Dawa. We ate together happily, with no Westerners in sight, and I felt that a sense of pride and bonding had now formed between us. We'd stood by each other. All the hard work and risks we'd taken together had paid off, and we were now in pole position for the summit. I wondered if this would be the true turning point I'd been seeking with Ed. Hopefully, it was the end of him seeing me as just some gobshite ex-Special Forces guy that he'd been paid to follow up the mountain. These kinds of psychological signs and signals are so subtle that it's hard to know how much is real and how much is in your head, but he certainly seemed more relaxed and enthusiastic in my company than before.

Just before 8 p.m. I decided to turn in for bed. As I stood to go, Ed asked me once again about the supplementary oxygen.

'Maybe you should do without it, see how you get on.'

'Yeah, I'll give it a go maybe and see how far I can get,' I replied, vaguely.

'No, but seriously, I really think you should.'

I couldn't deny it would be a major achievement for me and would put me in the company of some seriously elite

269

mountaineers. Compared with many people that I'd seen on this mountain, I was already breezing this. I thought back to that moment at 5 Hertford Street with Ivan. If I was going to make this trip count and tame my warrior ghost, I'd need to find the edge. Although nothing about this climb had been exactly easy, I'd yet to feel pushed to my limits. Ed knew this. Perhaps that was why he was so keen to see me climb without oxygen. Perhaps he wanted me to be tested. Was that what all this was really about? I didn't want to go down that negative trail of thought. I pushed my doubts aside and tried to take him at face value.

'Don't worry, mate,' I said, 'I'm on it. I'm thinking about it.'

'I know you could do it, Ant,' he said. 'You're a fucking machine.'

THE NEXT MORNING there was no way we were going anywhere, with or without oxygen. At 6 a.m. I was standing outside my tent staring up at the mountain. You could tell just by looking up at it that the conditions on top were terrible. There were gale-force winds, heavy snowfall, and the clouds around the summit were being whisked about as if by a mixer. Camp II was still like a ghost town, and most of the Sherpas from the different expedition companies gathered in huddles and engaged in intense conversation. Word had it that the fixing team was hoping to make it to the summit in a couple of days. There was no point in us climbing up to Camp III or IV, beneath the worst of that weather, and waiting with them. We had decent food right where we were, and all the physical and mental benefits of being at a lower altitude.

We awoke the following day to find the weather was still against us. Worse, we'd been joined by dozens of climbers who'd obviously negotiated the icefall the previous night, when conditions at the lower altitudes had been acceptable. If we weren't careful we were going to lose our advantage completely. All that risk would be rendered worthless and we'd be stuck in logjams the whole way up. I frantically thought of a new plan and ran it past Ed.

'Do we go up as high as the fixing team, and then, as soon as they've finished, go for the summit?'

'We don't want to piss them off,' he replied. 'It's not fair to give them that pressure. It's not really the done thing.'

'All right,' I said. 'But what if we went as high as Camp III and parked there? We'll be out of their hair. Then, as soon as they've fixed to the summit, we can go to IV and then do it? If we time it so we arrive at Camp IV at about 4 p.m., we could leave for the summit at ten or eleven that evening.'

'But what if they don't fix on that day?' said Ed. 'Then we'll be in stuck in Camp III for two days. Maybe more. That won't be a good idea. It'll make us weaker.'

Luckily for us, that year's fixing team was made up of Sherpas who'd been hired by Madison Mountaineering.

That meant Dawa, who was also with Madison, was able to get some extra intelligence on their progress. He discovered that they still didn't know when they'd be ready because the weather reports were too conflicting. Also, they didn't want us right on their heels but said they didn't mind if we stayed twelve hours behind them. The risk with this plan was that if we went up there and the weather at the summit didn't improve, it meant we'd be stuck at dangerously high altitudes for forty-eight hours or more. I decided to take that risk.

At 8 o'clock the next morning, as we launched into the arduous climb from Camp II to Camp III, morale was high. It was only as I was scaling the vast ice slopes of the Lhotse Face that it hit me that this challenge wasn't simply about getting to the summit. After working ourselves to a state of near exhaustion, we'd have to get back down as well. If anything, that might be an even tougher technical challenge. Reversing down the Lhotse Face was much more difficult because it's so unnatural. The human body isn't designed to travel backwards. Not only that, but we'd have all the ascending Biggerbollockses to cope with. Although we'd so far timed our climb perfectly by getting past the storm and leaving the others lower down the mountain, there would be no avoiding it. We'd be encountering them soon enough, whether we liked it or not.

We arrived at Camp III early in the afternoon. Ed and I climbed into our two-man tent for a short rest. We hadn't been inside for more than a few minutes when he brought up his idea yet again.

'So, what do you think about doing it without oxygen?'

I could tell that Ed was excited to see me pushed to my limits, but it felt a little like he was goading me. I remembered that feeling I'd got, back when we first met in the airport car park in Kathmandu and I'd had to subtly but firmly let him know that I was in charge. In that moment I could imagine him thinking, 'That's what you reckon, mate. Just wait until you're up that mountain. You're going to be running to me for help. I'm going to be taking care of you.' But then, when we got there, I was the one who was pushing him.

And then there was the avalanche, ten minutes after we'd emerged from the icefall. He'd put his camera on me and given it the old 'That could've been us, Ant.' And I'd told him, straightforwardly, that it wasn't. So it didn't bother me. I'd refused to play along with the 'I'm scared' cliché, and that was probably getting to him as well. I was beginning to suspect that all this about the oxygen was Ed – consciously or unconsciously – looking for a way to put me back in my place.

The truth was, I'd nearly gone for it. I'd taken his bait onto my tongue and given it a taste. Claiming the summit without supplementary oxygen on my first bid would be quite the achievement, and I was extremely tempted. But there was something about his frequent insistence that I do it that made me pause. Ed was trying to chip into me in any way he could, just to regain a little bit of control. I couldn't allow it. I had to retain my command. I couldn't allow myself to be sidetracked or dictated to by a situation or another person. After all, what was my goal here? What did I want? I'd never set out to do this without oxygen.

That was when I realised my mistake. For me, the temptation of summiting without oxygen wasn't about pride. It was about bragging rights. Being one of the few. It was, in other words, about my oldest and most tenacious foe – ego. I was furious with myself. How could I have even considered it? What I know now – but didn't then – is that it would have killed me. There is no doubt whatsoever that if I'd allowed ego to have dictated my decision on that mountain I'd never have walked off it. Being able to venture into the death zone without using supplementary oxygen is considered to be largely about an individual's genetics – many of the best mountaineers in the world simply cannot function at these heights without it – and as I'd never been so high before, I had no idea what was actually waiting for me up there and how I'd perform. The fact is, if I'd listened to my ego, my wife would be raising a family without a father.

All this made me angry, but what I didn't need now was an altercation. Although it's all very well being unafraid of conflict, it's also wise to know when to fight battles and when it's wiser to delay them. Strategy is crucial and, for now, it was vitally important that relations stay positive and morale high.

'Mate,' I said gently, 'I want to push as hard as I can without oxygen, but I don't think I'll be allowed to because of Channel 4, insurance-wise,' I said.

'Well, that hasn't stopped you trying to tackle the mountain through massive fucking storms,' he said. 'So why would that be an issue now?'

'I called into the office when I was in Namche. I'm not signed off to do it.'

This was not true. I hoped my little white lie would be enough to put him off. I watched him chew on it for a moment.

'Nobody can tell you what to do up here, mate,' he said. 'You can do what you want. Come on, man, why would you let that lot back in London tell you what to do?'

I felt my blood lurch. This was beginning to piss me off.

'Ed, you've summited three times,' I said. 'Have you ever done it without oxygen?'

'I haven't,' he said. 'But I'm not Ant Middleton. I reckon you should think about it. Seriously.'

Twenty minutes later, Dawa was fitting me with my oxygen tank. And then we were off again, climbing towards Camp IV into what looked like better weather. The snow was deep, the gradient steep and I'd never felt so weak. It was as if my superpowers had been ripped away from me. At that altitude, where there's only a third of the oxygen that's in the lowlands, the human body is slowly dying, and I was convinced I could actually feel it happening. With every step I felt I was being suffocated. It was as if all the weight of Everest itself was pushing down on me, throttling me, squeezing the air from my lungs and the blood from my muscles.

When we arrived at the edge of the death zone at around 3 p.m., I drew a sense of grim satisfaction that it did look exactly as a death zone should. Camp IV on Everest's South Col was a picture of lifelessness, of barren sterility. Just under 8,000 metres up, we were surrounded by abandoned oxygen tanks and destroyed tents, many of them decades old. The weather reports were saying that our summit day would be the best in five seasons, with the skies clear and the wind at a pleasant five to ten knots.

'This is brilliant news,' I told Ed. 'It's all worked out perfectly. We've got seven hours to have a lie down and get our heads in gear before our final assault on the summit.'

Back in our little two-man tent, Ed and I prepared a couple of small portions of ramen noodles. We ate them with considerable effort, then shut our headtorches off and climbed inside our sleeping bags. I don't know how long I lay there in the dark. Eventually I heard Ed turn over and clear his throat uncomfortably.

'How you feeling, Ed?'

'I can't sleep, man.'

'Neither can I.'

'How long have we got?'

I looked at my watch. 'Two hours. We've got to get some sleep.'

'Aye. Roger that.'

But it was impossible. The nerves, the excitement, the discomfort and the roar of the wind made anything like proper rest completely impossible. Finally, 10 p.m. rolled around.

'Let's do this,' I said.

On went our headtorches again, piercing the pitch black. I unzipped my –40°C-rated sleeping bag and stood out of it, fastened up my summit suit that I'd not bothered to remove, then we began the process of sorting out all our kit, putting on our harnesses and double-checking each other. Once we were out of the tent, we fastened our crampons, checked each other over once more, pulled our hoods up and tested our oxygen regulators. In the daysack on my back, as well as my oxygen tank, I had a twenty-four-hour survival kit, including extra warm gloves, ice screws, extra carabiners, a small camera and spare batteries. I looked at Ed. I looked at Dawa. Ed and Dawa looked at me.

'Is everyone good to go?'

And, with that, we were off into the abyss.

* * *

WE HAD A hell of a journey ahead of us to climb to the summit and then, if we reached it, to get back down to Camp IV. Fifteen hours in all, at first up perilous slopes and mostly in the dark, the light from our headtorches falling every now and then across the corpses of once strong men and women, who looked as fresh as yesterday.

I soon realised that my feet were freezing, despite all my layers. I tried to push the worry out of my head, but it was difficult. The fact is that humans simply weren't designed to survive at these altitudes. We were about to climb to nearly the cruising height of a Boeing 747. I knew that in all likelihood I wasn't just suffering from the cold but that I had some sort of circulation problem. 'When I get moving a bit more they'll warm up,' I told myself. But they didn't. Four hours into our climb we arrived at the small ledge at 8,400 metres known as the Balcony. By then it had begun to feel as if someone had wrapped thin cotton thread around the base of each one of my toes and was pulling on the ends as hard as they could. With every step I took, I kicked them hard into the ground in an attempt to force some feeling into them. But it was just sheer agony. I confided to Ed what was happening.

'You might lose your toes,' he told me.

'Yeah, I know, I've been thinking about that,' I said. 'But I'm willing to make that sacrifice.'

'Are you sure?'

'Yeah. There's no way I'm giving up.'

I was happy to lose a few toes. I could always get fake ones. Imagine turning around four hundred metres below the summit of Everest because I'd – literally – got cold feet.

Before we left for the final push, Dawa took out some energy bars for us to snack on. Even in the box in his pack they'd become frozen. He snapped a piece off and put it in my mouth, but it was too hard to eat. The boiling water in his Thermos flask had gone cold. I sipped as much as I could before sliding my mask back on with shaking fingers and telling them, 'Let's just crack on.' We continued in single file, with Dawa leading the way and Ed behind me. I wanted to maintain the pace and keep my blood flowing, because I was desperate to keep my feet as warm as possible.

And then there was light. From being an ocean of black, the sky became illuminated with a strange red-orange ring of light that completely surrounded us, like one of Saturn's rings. It was breathtaking. Heavenly. We'd finally broken out of the darkness. I suddenly felt myself becoming emotional. Tears were welling up. I put my head down and had a word with myself: 'Ant, what are you doing? You're not on the summit yet. Save it.' I didn't know it then, but I'd just enjoyed my happiest moment on the mountain.

From the South Summit there's an hour or two of ascent still to go, including the sheer climb of the Hillary Step and then, at long last, the true summit. There was only one route in, along the rope that the fixing team had laid for us, onto which we were now clipped. The gradients were incredibly steep, the track narrow and slippery. If you unclipped from the rope and slipped, even a little, you were dead.

To my shock and irritation, as we rounded a corner I saw a line of other climbers – perhaps twenty-five of them – ahead of me. A whole expedition's worth. I couldn't believe it. They must have left Camp IV a few hours before us while we were still trying to get some rest. As I approached them I realised that one man in a bright yellow summit suit was lagging behind. He seemed to be struggling to breathe, even with the help of his supplementary oxygen. He didn't look fit to be up there.

I wasn't prepared to wait. I decided to take the risk of unclipping from the fixed rope and trying to move past him before clipping back on. In order to do that I'd need him to stop moving for a minute, otherwise he'd be liable to knock into me and send me tumbling. But when I asked, he ignored me. I tried remonstrating with his Sherpas but that only made him turn on them.

'Help me!' he started shouting at them. 'Help me!'

I had no idea what he expected them to do. As far as he was concerned, he'd paid his money to summit Everest and that meant they had to practically put him on their backs. It was obvious, from their expressions, that they hated him.

I turned back to Ed and shouted over my shoulder, 'Let's get past this idiot here.'

I clipped off and took the risk of walking a little bit past him as he writhed about, his feet slipping, his arms flailing.

I walked gingerly for about ten metres then clipped back into the rope. I looked up. A few steps more and this seven-and-a-half-hour climb would be over. I'd be there.

And then, there I was, on that black rock pyramid at the highest point on earth. One foot in Tibet, one in Nepal. I'd noticed that the visibility had started becoming worse about fifteen minutes earlier. Now it had deteriorated quite significantly. But I wasn't too disappointed. I hadn't done this for the view. I allowed myself a moment of proud reflection. If only that young lad on Snowdon could see me now. Before I left there was one more thing I had to do. I lifted the satellite phone out from my pack and with thick, shaking gloved fingers called Emilie.

'Hello?'

'Ant,' she said. 'Is that you?'

'Just to let you know, I'm standing on top of the world.'

I couldn't help it. I began tearing up again.

'Thanks to you and the kids for always being there for me. I love you millions. I love you more than you'll ever know.'

'I love you too, Ant,' she said. 'Well done, my love. You're amazing.' She went quiet for a moment. 'Ant – are you all right? I can hear there's a lot of wind up there. Is there a storm?'

'No, no.' I looked around me. 'The wind's just come in now.'

'You'd better go,' she said.

'OK. I love you. Bye.'

Putting the phone away, I realised that Emilie was right. I was in a whiteout. The wind had picked up fiercely and I could now see almost nothing but snow. It was coming down so fast and so fine it was starting to get everywhere, up in my cuffs and down the back of my neck. I blinked, inside my goggles, and found that my eyelashes had started to freeze over. I glanced up at Ed, who'd been filming my phone call. He looked concerned.

'My camera's going down,' he said. 'We need to get off the mountain. Fast.'

I knew he was right.

But the problem was, it wasn't just me who was on the summit of Everest. I was just one of about twenty-five others, who'd been busy taking selfies and doing group hugs. I had a sudden flashback to that waypoint back down in the Khumbu with its 50,000 recorded trekkers in a single year. Once again, I didn't feel very special. I wanted to be the highest man in the world. Officially. Just me and me alone. Nobody else in sight. I wanted the rest of them gone. Only then I could have my rightful moment.

'You go ahead, mate,' I said. 'I'll catch you up.'

That was my mistake.

CHAPTER 12

EVERYONE'S SECRET FEAR

SO FAR WE'VE explored three different varieties of fear, each of which comes with its own particular set of quirks and dangers. The big three fears – of suffering, failure and conflict – all have the power to give us sticky boots and root us to the spot, keeping us in the same corridor, turning us negative, making us shrink. Different people experience these fears at different levels. I saw the fear of suffering negatively affect the performance of countless people on Everest as they got stuck in their fear bubbles for too long, paralysed by 'Maybe' and unable to find the courage to commit. Then came Biggerbollocks, Ferris and many others like them, who were motivated by ego rather than pride, caught up in the fear of other people classing them as failures. Finally, there are all the people whose ultimate goal is to be popular and so fail to progress because they're terrified of interpersonal conflict.

But what if I were to tell you that underneath the big three is actually just one ultimate fear that drives them all? What if it turns out that all of these fears are actually the same?

It was a young woman in Liverpool who really showed me the surprising truth about human fear. I met her after a show. I'd run off stage and leapt into the car that had been waiting, and it tore off through the dark city streets while the audience at the theatre was still applauding. As we drove, I noticed that a vehicle seemed to be tailing us. A purple Kia had been parked up on the double yellows a few yards away from the backstage door, and it was now following us around every twist and turn. I was on guard, but I wasn't worried. There aren't many genuine threats that come bursting out of a purple Kia.

When we reached the hotel and pulled up outside the entrance, the Kia parked up ten metres away. I got out of my car slightly warily. Two women that I'd never met before popped out of the Kia. It seemed a lot of effort to go to just to get a selfie. I waited in the cold as they trotted up. As they got closer I noticed that one of them was clutching a copy of my last book, *First Man In*. Sticking out of its pages were dozens of little Post-It notes. The woman with the book looked to be in her early thirties and had long, dark hair. She was underdressed for the weather and I could see goosebumps on her knees, although wearing hardly any clothes on a night out in winter is standard operating procedure for anyone living north of Birmingham.

'All right?' I said. 'Been busy reading?'

'You've changed my way of thinking,' she said. 'You've changed everything.'

As opening gambits go, this was pretty intense.

'Okay,' I said. 'In a good way, I hope.'

'I can't believe I've met you. Oh my God. I don't feel worthy.'

'Not worthy? What a thing to say. Who's told you you're not worthy?'

'But I'm not worthy,' she said. 'I'm nothing. I'm just a till girl in Morrisons.'

'Nothing? You've just told me I've changed your way of thinking. If you're calling yourself nothing, I can't have changed it that much.'

She told me her name was Kayleigh. There was something about the way she was talking, and how her mate was taking a diplomatic step back and letting her rattle on, that made me suspect that there was a deeper reason why she wanted to talk to me so badly than just a selfie and a signed book. I didn't want to give her the wrong idea by asking her in for a drink, so I invited her for a quick chat in the hotel lobby. After we'd found a quiet place to sit down, I decided to continue the small talk so I could see where it was going.

'And is that where you're happy working? Morrisons?'

'Not really,' she said nervously.

'So why don't you apply to college? Work towards something better?'

It was clear the idea had never even occurred to her.

'College?' she said. 'Oh my God, I could never do college.'

'Why not?'

She thought for a moment.

'I just couldn't.'

'You're scared,' I told her. 'You're frightened of moving on.'

'I'm not scared,' she said. 'I just know my limitations.'

'You've got absolutely no idea about your limitations,' I said. 'I can tell that just by what you've said. You've got no idea how much potential you've got.'

With that, she burst into tears.

'Listen, don't cry,' I told her. 'Just listen to me for a sec. Do you know how I know you've got no idea about your limitations? You don't know what your limits are because you're not testing them. You're not pushing them. You're not even going anywhere near them. You're huddled in the back of your cave, too scared to stray anywhere near the entrance. Within seconds of meeting me you said you were "nothing". What a load of rubbish. Nobody is "nothing". Why do you think you're "nothing"? What made you say it?'

And then it all came tumbling out. Kayleigh told me she was adopted and, when she was fourteen, had somehow found out that her biological mother had kept all her other kids – and not her. This, she believed, had traumatised her. It had damaged her. It had made her believe she was worthless. And now she was living in a flat with her alcoholic foster sister and paying all the rent. She refused to consider college because that would mean downsizing, and her foster sister would be furious as she'd have to find somewhere else to live and maybe wouldn't forgive her. Kayleigh was scared of dealing with that conflict and didn't think she could handle it. She was also scared of suffering, because if she became a student she'd have even less money, and that would be tough. And she was scared of failure, of not succeeding in higher education. The big three were all there, each one coating her unseasonal high heels in layers and layers of glue. But underneath them all was one single fear: 'I'm not good enough.'

Talking her situation through, I came to realise that this one fear – 'I'm not good enough' – was actually her only fear. If she could solve that one, she could solve them all. She *was* good enough to handle that conflict with her foster sister. She *was* good enough to cope with having less money for a while. She *was* good enough to gain a qualification from college. So why did she believe she wasn't good enough in the first place? Because her default mindset was using her memories against her. It was searching around in her past and trying to define her in the present in order to keep her in the place that seemed safe. It was nothing more than chatter. And if she didn't learn to overcome that chatter, she'd be kept glued in that same corridor forever. She would shrink.

YOU ARE KAYLEIGH
FROM LIVERPOOL

This might sound unlikely, but it's absolutely true. You are Kayleigh from Liverpool. We all are. 'I'm not good enough' is the ultimate human fear. Look underneath each one of the big three, and this is what you'll find. Some of us fear we haven't got what it takes to cope with suffering. Some of us fear we haven't got what it takes to achieve our goals and that others will realise the 'truth' that we're 'failures'. Some of us fear we don't have what it takes to handle conflict. And powering every single one of these fears? 'I'm not good enough.' It's everyone's secret fear.

Where does this universal fear come from? How do you experience it? Just as with Kayleigh, it comes at us as part of that negative chatter. You hear it in your head. You approach a door of opportunity and the fear floods into you. Then the default mindset kicks in because it wants to keep you safe, and that's when the chatter begins. It drowns you in arguments as to why you shouldn't step through that door, listing all the reasons it's not safe and making every single worst-case scenario seem inevitable. It all sounds completely convincing.

But in actual fact, every single argument it's making is just another version of 'You're not good enough.' That voice wants you to believe it's your greatest ally, but it's really your worst enemy – and you should treat it as such. Rather than listening to it and humbly abiding by its message, you should make that voice your energy. Get angry at it. It's an evil parent. Prove to that negative opponent – who wants nothing more than to keep you stuck and fearful in your safe corridor – that it's wrong.

The simple fact is, you don't know if you're good enough until you open that door. And even then, maybe things on the other side of it won't be as you'd hoped. At the very least, you'll have learned something new and be better prepared for your next attempt. Your failure, in that moment, does not determine who you are. The critical thing to remember is this: you might think that you're defined by your tally of successes and failures. I'm here to tell you that you're not. There's no list in existence that itemises what's gone right in your life and what's gone wrong, and then makes a final calculation that tells you who you are.

What actually defines you is your capacity for opening doors. If you're always stuck in that same corridor, listening to the negative chatter that's telling you that you're not good enough, then you're shrinking. Your life is going into retreat. But if you're smashing through those doors – even if a lot of the time you're falling flat on your face – you're nobody's loser. You're living. Keep on at it. Keep accruing those scars and calluses. Keep learning those lessons. You'll grow. You'll succeed. It's inevitable.

PROVE THAT YOU'RE GOOD ENOUGH A HUNDRED TIMES A DAY

All fear comes from not having sufficient trust in yourself. When people get stuck in a cycle of doubting themselves, it usually comes from years of being told 'You can't do this, you can't do that' by well-meaning parents and teachers. Unfortunately, this is not a problem that's going away any time soon. We're living in an era of massively overprotective helicopter parenting that's creating a generation of fearful, negative people.

If you feel that your fear of not being good enough is holding you back and getting you stuck in the same corridor, then I'd encourage you to put yourself on a daily programme of proving to that negative voice in your head that it's wrong. If the definition of success is overcoming challenge, then the good news is that everyday life is filled with hundreds of little challenges. I'm constantly challenging everything I do. Even tiny things like putting the bins out before I leave the house or neatening up a pair of shoes when I get in – I don't want to do these things, and that's what makes them a challenge. I genuinely feel a little hit of pride every time I overcome my resistance and take the time to complete these micro-tasks. Each tiny victory is another 'Fuck you' to that negative chatter in my head.

This is how I live my life. It happens every time I walk to the station. I might have plenty of time to take a pleasant stroll down and grab a coffee on the way, but I race myself. 'The last time I did this in eighteen minutes,' I'll think, 'but this time I'll do it in seventeen.' Then when I get to the station, sweating in my big winter coat and with nothing to do but hang around on the freezing platform for twenty minutes, I'll tell myself, 'You bloody idiot'. But I can't help it. When I get to the tube I'll find myself thinking, 'Why are you taking the escalator when you could be taking the stairs? Why are you walking slow when you could be walking fast?' I'll tip up to important meetings covered in sweat – and I'm an hour early, so I have to sit in a café anyway. One voice says to me, 'Ant, slow down, mate. Chill out.' But then there's always another voice that replies, 'Chill out? Why, when you can have this little achievement?'

If the default mindset is 'You're not good enough,' the positive mindset is 'I'm better than I was yesterday.' This is the attitude you should be cultivating. From the moment you wake up, set yourself a challenge, even if it's a small one, like making sure your bed is made before you leave the house. Put yourself in the correct frame of mind and challenge yourself constantly – you can prove to yourself that you're 'good enough' one hundred times a day.

WHEN FEAR TAKES OVER

Sadly there are huge numbers of people out there who will read what I've just recommended and think it's completely unimaginable. Even the micro-tasks, like putting the bins out and neatening up your shoes. To these men and women, a positive daily life filled with little challenges that have been successfully overcome feels like an utter physical and mental impossibility. Almost every day I'm contacted by someone suffering from serious depression, someone who sees the world in a completely different way to me and is convinced that reality is filled with enormous obstacles they couldn't possibly leap.

I met just such an individual during my recent tour. It was ten minutes from showtime and my tour manager knocked on my dressing-room door.

'There's someone outside that wants to see you,' he said. 'A father with his teenage son.'

'Mate, I'm just about to go on stage.'

'He just wants a five-minute chat. The kid lost his best buddy a couple of months ago and he's not dealing with it very well. He's got exams coming up and he's fallen into a rut over the last couple of months. That's what his dad says, anyway.'

How could I say no to that? As my tour manager exited, in walked the father and the depressed fourteen-year-old.

The dad seemed quite excited to be there, but the boy was hanging back, looking vacant and disinterested.

'How are you, mate?' I asked him.

'Could be better.'

'I hear you've just lost your best friend.'

He nodded.

'By the looks of it, you're at risk of losing yourself.'

He met my eye for the first time.

'It's hard to deal with. I can't process it.'

'So what happened to him?'

'He hit his head. Fell off some scaffolding.'

'And that wasn't your fault, was it?'

'I wasn't even there.'

'So put yourself in your mate's shoes,' I said. 'Imagine he's in the room now seeing the effect his death has had on you. He doesn't want this, does he? I understand why you're grieving. You and him were best friends. But you're not doing his death any justice. You need to make him proud of you. When my father passed away I went through three years of hell. And then I looked at myself and realised he must be turning in his grave seeing me going out of my mind fighting, drinking, turning into the man he'd never have wanted me to be – and all because of something that was out of my control. Yes, we all go through the process of grief. But you need to acknowledge what's happened, process it and move on. He doesn't want you to honour him with sadness. He doesn't want to be responsible for destroying you. He wants you to honour him by living a life for the both of you. So that's what you need to do now.'

After talking him through my 'acknowledge, process, move on' method, I had a quiet word with his father. It turned out that the kid was struggling even to get out of bed. His dad was worried that he was becoming suicidal, and I suspected that he was probably correct. The whole world had become one gigantic fear bubble for his boy.

'Listen,' I said, 'the only way he's going to pull himself out of this rut is by slowly turning his mindset around. He needs to go from "everything is impossible" to "nothing is impossible". You can make this happen for him by giving him one challenge at a time and allowing it to make one positive impact at a time.'

The way to do this, I explained, was to make mini fear bubbles for him to step into and successfully burst. 'Start small, but be brutal about it,' I told him. On day one, his only challenge might be to put all his clothes away. 'Tell him he's got all day. Eight hours. But he has to do it. Once he's in that bubble and has committed by picking up his first shirt, he's in. He'll complete the job. And then he can get back in bed and enjoy what he's done. Look at it. Feel good about it. That's the first chip in his wall of negativity. The next day, give him something else to do. But take it slowly. Allow him to feel good about his little victories.'

It was about giving him a tiny sense of achievement that he could build on, slowly breaking down his belief that reality itself was one massive fear bubble. It was about proving to him, slowly but surely, that the ultimate fear of 'I'm not good enough to get through this' was simply wrong. Since my encounter with that man and his son, I've given this same advice to at least twenty people who were suffering from serious depression. All the feedback I've had about the technique has been overwhelmingly positive. At the time of writing, I'm incredibly proud to be able to say that three people have got back in touch and credited it with saving their lives.

YOU ARE NOT YOUR PAST

When people fail to learn to harness fear, one of the reasons you hear time and time again is that they can't succeed because of some trauma. The basic idea is that if something bad happened to you in the past, then that thing is a block on your performance in the present. But a calm, clear look at reality will tell you that this simply isn't true. You can take anyone who's stuck in their corridor and blames the bullying they once suffered or domestic violence they once witnessed – and then find someone else who experienced events that were ten times as bad and yet became ten times as successful. The world is full of people who haven't let memories of long-gone events hold them back. The proof that we're not defined by our past is everywhere to see.

The fact is, pretty much every one of us can find something in our past that was traumatic – and I'm no exception. Everyone has a memory of violence being committed upon them. Everyone has a memory of being abandoned. Everyone has a memory of being victimised and treated horrendously. If you're looking for evidence of unfairness in your life, you'll find it. If you're looking for evidence of your victim status, you'll find it. And if you don't find it in your own past, you'll find it in the past of your ancestors, or your ancestors' ancestors, and then hold that up as a reason for your inability to actually take responsibility for your life and grow. We all have excuses we can pull out. And why do we pull them out? Because that negative chatter is always looking for a way to excuse our lack of courage. Appeals to the bad events in the past are perfect – they somehow make us feel like brave heroes even as we're allowing ourselves to be swallowed up by fear.

Past trauma is no reason for current failure. It's only since the advent of psychotherapy that we've been encouraged to root around in our childhoods and dig out possible causes for our lack of success. But, aside from extreme examples of childhood abuse and neglect, these are usually little more than convenient excuses. When we're not brave enough to open doors, we'll do anything but admit that the problem is a simple lack of courage. The default mindset doesn't want us taking responsibility for our lives. So we pat ourselves on the back and tell ourselves that the problem is our victimhood. We demand that people treat us as special, simply because something bad once happened.

But this is simply not true. It's just chatter. It's that default mindset trying to send you back under the covers where it thinks you'll be safe. And that's exactly where you *will* be if you listen to it – under the covers, depressed and stuck and shrinking. You don't look backwards to walk forwards. It's only once you fully grasp the fact that all these negative thoughts about you being 'damaged' or 'not good enough' are just chatter that you'll have the capacity to become limitless.

Forget the past. You can't change it. It has no power over you. And forget the future too. You can't control that either. You can only change your life in the present. All that matters is right now.

TRUE FAILURE COMES BUT ONCE

It wasn't until I joined the Special Forces that I really learned the extent to which our memories of the past can needlessly hold us back. Back when I'd been a member of the Paras and Marines, I still struggled to find the correct motivation in my life. I was too concerned with what everyone else thought of me. I had a fear of not being accepted, of not belonging somewhere. That's why I jumped around so much. But then

I passed Selection. When I was presented with that beret and belt I was filled with pride for my own achievements. It was the first time in my life that I thought, 'I'm exactly where I'm supposed to be. All the trials and tribulations and painful incidents that took place before this, you can now leave behind. Chapter closed.'

I realised that I'd sometimes been guilty of clinging on to all the bad things that had happened to me like you'd hang on to the side of a life raft. I kept on judging myself by all the negative things that had occurred, and I'd sometimes allowed those events to become an excuse. I'd think, 'Well, of course you didn't pull that one off. You're the guy who quit the green army, you're the guy who got kicked out of the police force for drink driving.' It was too easy just to class myself as a failure by only looking back at those things in my life that hadn't gone to plan – and then letting myself off the hook. 'Just look at all the times you've failed in the past, mate. What did you expect?'

But when I really thought about it, I realised that even when I'd 'failed', I hadn't really failed. Because success or failure is never black and white. Just because things haven't gone as you'd hoped or predicted, it doesn't mean that you've lost. There are people who have served thirty years in prison or suffered from paralysis or a serious disease who'll tell you that they wouldn't change a thing. Why? Because they understand that they've become better people as a result of the trials they've gone through. Show me someone who has never suffered or failed, and I'll show you a spoiled, weak, useless individual who has nothing interesting to say for themselves. The whole point of lessons is that they're tough. You can call that 'failure' if you want. I call it life.

The 'failure' that your default mindset chatter wants you to believe in is a binary one. It's a yes or a no, a tick or a cross, a black or a white. It wants you to believe that because it's trying to stop you from stepping into fear bubbles and opening doors. It thinks it's keeping you safe. Yes, if you put yourself out through that door, things might happen that you wouldn't necessarily choose. You might lose a contract, you might make an enemy, you might look like an idiot for ten minutes. But if you don't go through it, your chances of success in life are zero. Life is not a series of right or wrong choices. You don't pop that fear bubble and get a black or a white. It's not pure good or pure bad on the other side of that door. It's a new world. It might not be the world you've imagined or even hoped for, but only by stepping into it do you become a new and better you.

The only time you're ever going to get a black and white result from opening a door is if you're struck down dead. I've walked through doors that held that intense level of threat more times than I can count. But unless your business is violent crime, serious contact sports or the military, you're practically never going to be confronted by such doors. And if you are? Dying is just a matter of timing. You're not going to avoid it forever. It's going to happen. And the good news is, every other door that you ever step through in life is not going to lead to you being killed. And if you're suddenly taken out? You probably won't know a single thing about it. Death is the easiest thing you'll ever have to do. So, what is there to be afraid of?

CHAPTER 13

REVENGE OF THE KING

THERE I WAS, alone, the undisputed king of the world. With the end of my gloved forefinger I touched the tip of the pole that rises out of Mount Everest's summit and revelled in my crowning moment. I had barely a moment to enjoy it. Ed had departed just five minutes earlier and the members of the large expedition that had also made it to the top had followed closely behind him. Even in this brief period the weather had begun bearing down with even greater force. By now the wind had started blasting into my side at around sixty knots, and waves of fine snow had begun slashing at my face and torso.

I pulled up my hood and headed down, walking as briskly as my weakened, heavy legs were able to take me along the ridge towards the Hillary Step, with Dawa just behind me. For the past eight hours my feet had been nothing but weighty bricks of deadness and pain. By the time I was out of this I wasn't sure if I would keep any of my toes. Just being up there in the first place with my ragged feet would have counted as a dangerous situation. Throw in the unexpected storm that was now buffeting, blinding and deafening me, and I couldn't begin to calculate my odds of getting down safely. What was the point in even trying? The most important thing now was to try to get off the mountain as quickly as possible in order to breathe thicker air, thaw out and find medical attention.

Because my hood was up and I was concentrating on where I was putting my feet, I didn't see the man in front of me. The first I knew anyone was there at all was when I made sudden physical contact with him, banging into his shoulder and arm. What the hell was going on? We were in a world of danger here, so why wasn't this idiot moving? I blinked my eyes into focus and looked past him. All I could see, disappearing into the blizzard of fine snow, was a long line of people. Nobody seemed to be moving. What was happening? This was insane. We had to get off the mountain. We had to get off *now*.

The problem seemed to be that the wild conditions were proving too much for the nerves of these relatively inexperienced climbers. They were lined up at the top of the Hillary Step, panicking not only about the necessity of having to unclip from the rope to get past the anchor point that holds the rope in place at the Step's lip, but also about the descent itself, which was now having to be tackled in extremely high winds. I made a rapid count of how many people were in front of me, then roughly multiplied this by how long it was taking each person to complete the manoeuvre. As I struggled in my attempt to do the maths, I noticed the behaviour of the Sherpas who were guiding the expedition that was causing all these problems. They were shouting, 'Move! Move! We need to move!' The Westerners in front of me were beginning to visibly panic, some of them now shouting as well and straining to look ahead. At some point later I eventually finished calculating the numbers. Two hours. I was going to be up here, waiting, for two hours.

It was over. I was a dead man. There was no question about it. Nobody could survive extreme whiteout conditions in the death zone for two hours. It simply wasn't possible.

I felt the blood sink from my head and gather itself in a heavy pool around my gut. My legs felt suddenly weaker. I began to go into a negative spiral. Because it was ego, wasn't it? My oldest enemy. It was ego that had made me want to feel like the 'undisputed king of the world' and stand on the summit alone. Well, here was the mountain reminding me who the real king was, just as it had reminded hundreds of doomed souls before me. I remembered what I'd told Emilie all those months ago, back there in the impossible warmth and safety of my kitchen. This was going to be a camping trip. A walk in the park. I was so much more capable than your average Everest tourist that I'd be able to do it backwards. My training package could consist of red wine and room-service chicken wings. I could spend four days in Namche on the piss. What was it I always told people? You should be motivated by pride, not by ego. It's ego that gets you killed. Well, congratulations, Ant Middleton. You're about to prove your point. Some time within the next hour you're going to become just another waymarker for next year's climbers, like Green Boots and all the others, a permanently frozen monument to the truth of your own fucking lesson.

I had to get a grip of myself. I had to work out what this was and what it wasn't. Well, I wasn't dead yet. I was alive right now and that was all that mattered. If I met a negative situation with negative thinking, then negative would be all I could ever hope to get back. Behind me I noticed that Dawa had pulled himself down in a little ball and leaned back against the snow. I decided to do the same, shuffling up the queue whenever the next person found the courage to go. I was feeling colder and colder, any sensation in my feet now a distant memory, aside from the burning rims of pain around my toes.

Down in my little ball on the ground I somehow managed to huddle myself into a pocket of warmth. I was tired and weak but, for the first time in a long time, I was actually feeling comfortable. Waves of restful calm flowed over me. You know, this wasn't too bad. I would just stay there like this and see the storm out. After a while I stopped wanting the queue to move up at all. The closer we got to the Step, the sooner I'd be forced to leave my safe, gorgeous and cosy sphere. I just wanted to stay there. I would rest. Sleep. Wake up when the sun returned, then descend at my leisure in the warmth of a brand new day. It was funny, because with my head buried deep into the crook of my arm I could actually see it in front of me. The blue sky. High and clear above me. Bright. Warm. Perfect. I was lifting into it. Lifting into it. Lighter and lighter and lighter and lighter.

I was dying. I wasn't close to dying. It was actually happening. My brain was shutting down. It was seducing me into a sleep from which I'd never awake. With a burst of fury I pushed myself to my feet and began kicking at the snow as hard as I could with the blocks of ice that were hanging off the bottom of my legs. The blizzard had now become more intense than ever, and thousands of pinpricks of snow were finding their way down the back of my neck and into the edges of my goggles. I gripped my hood and squeezed it shut around me, but still the snow was getting in. I felt another great wave of tiredness sweep over me and had to fight to stop myself getting back into that ball. I needed something to occupy my mind. In my front pockets were my big, comfortable mitts, while in my side pockets were my working gloves. It gave me an idea. I would start switching them – mitts on, gloves on, mitts on, gloves on – over and over and over again.

I must have changed them twenty times when another tempting thought occurred to me. I would keep my cosy mitts on for the rest of the climb down. I shuffled up one more place. 'Yeah, that's enough with my gloves now,' I thought. 'I'm going to go down the rope in my mitts.' There. It was decided.

But what was I thinking? In a moment of clarity I realised that it was the lack of oxygen that was getting to me. Even with the help of the tanks of our backs, climbers still didn't get as much oxygen as they were normally used to. After a while the impoverished air begins affecting the functions of the brain, hence my difficulty calculating a simple sum. The horror stories of Everest are filled with accounts of strong and experienced individuals becoming catastrophically confused or possessed by irrational ideas. 'No, no, no,' I told myself. 'Get a grip of yourself. You need your working gloves on.'

'I can't be arsed,' another voice inside me replied. 'I'm comfortable now. I'm warm.'

'You'll fucking die. You need the use of your fingers.'

IT WAS MORE than two and a half hours before Dawa and I finally reached the Step. When I got there I immediately saw what had been slowing us all down. As well as all the extra caution that each climber had been taking, there was a man at the edge who'd been overcome with fear and was failing to move. Before I reached him, people were just carefully unclipping past him and moving around. But just as my turn finally came, he decided to attempt the descent. Now I was close enough, I recognised who he was. It was the same man

I'd seen on the way up, who'd refused to let me pass him in safety. And there he was again, stuck and flailing. He was being bashed around in the wind like a rag doll.

'I can't see,' he shouted. 'I can't see where to put my feet.'

'Get this idiot down,' I told his Sherpas.

They were leaning over the ledge and began barking at him, 'Go down! Go down!'

'I can't see,' he shouted again. 'I can't see where to put my feet.'

One of the Sherpas leaned down and yanked up his goggles. His eyelashes were knitted together with dozens of tangled strands of ice. With a furious brutality, the Sherpa began using his rigid fingers to dig it all out of his eyes.

'OK, get down now,' he shouted. 'We are all going to die. You must get down.'

Finally, he disappeared from view. I clipped back onto the rope past the ice anchor and prepared to follow him down. Just as I was getting in position, I looked down and saw that he was still barely a metre beneath me, hanging upside down. The rope had somehow pinned him against the face and he couldn't move at all. The sight of him gave me a rush of sheer panic. 'Get a grip of your fucking mind, Ant,' I hissed to myself. 'You're not dead yet.'

I looked down again. The man wasn't struggling. He was completely still. Was he dead? After a second, he twitched to life and began flailing about like a caught fish. Then he faded again. He seemed to be drifting in and out of consciousness.

Up on the ridge beside me, his Sherpas began trying to pull him up, grabbing for him, but he was too far away from them to quite reach.

'What are we going to do?' I shouted.

'We're going to cut him off the mountain,' one of them said. He turned to Dawa, who was crouched behind. 'Do you have a knife?'

Dawa shook his head.

'Do you have a knife?' the Sherpa asked me.

I also shook my head. By now the second Sherpa was fumbling in his backpack. I saw a black handle emerge and the dull shine of the steel. This was it. The man was gone. I looked away. I didn't want to see it. I didn't want the memory of watching him vanish into the whiteness.

As I stared into the blank sky I became aware of a sudden burst of movement beneath me. I don't know if the man had heard the Sherpa's exchange and grasped what was about to happen, but he'd somehow found enough fight inside him to let off a final explosion of energy. I looked down to see that although he was still pinned to the mountain, he'd somehow managed to flip himself to a diagonal, force his arm through an old piece of fixed rope that looked like it had been there for years and pull himself up into a half-cocked position. But the main fixed rope was now strangling him.

Both his Sherpas were once again lying on their fronts, leaning dangerously over the edge, grabbing for him. Dawa was now helping them and they had enough leverage to pull him back up upright, the three of them managing to help him find his feet and kick them into the wall of ice. He was saved. I'll never know how, but he made it down the face.

I'll never know how I did it either. Watching him struggle planted a seed of doubt in me. I'd been waiting there for three hours and had never felt so vulnerable, even in combat zones with bullets flying over my head. There was now a huge fear bubble at the top of that descent. Worse, he'd loosened the rope. I steeled myself and stepped into the bubble, feeling its almost overwhelming force. *You've got this. You can do this.* I committed. Before I knew it, I'd negotiated my way unsteadily down, and Dawa and I were soon completely clear of the Hillary Step.

Fifty metres from the South Summit we hit another small queue of four or five people. As we shuffled closer through the fog of snow, I realised there was someone on a little ledge just up from the track whom they'd all stopped to talk to. When I drew close to him I could see that he looked like a Sherpa, a guy in his mid-thirties. He must have been helping people, I thought, counting them through. But then I saw that he was just sitting on the ledge, unclipped from the fixed rope, hugging his knees with his head down. He had no oxygen on.

'What's going on, mate?' I asked him

He peered up at me. 'I'm sleeping.'

'You can't fucking sleep here. You're going to die. What are you doing?'

'Leave me. I'm sleeping.'

I grabbed his arm and pulled him towards me. 'You need to get off the mountain.'

He shrugged me off. There was nothing I could do but let him lift off into his own perfect warm blue sky.

For the first time in my life I was leaving someone to their death. It was a truly horrific thing to have to do, and it will never leave me. But aside from my having no practical choice, my mindset was in pure survival mode. I couldn't stop to think any more about it. The fact is, if I'd tried to save him, neither of us would have come home.

Dawa and I shortly found ourselves in a place where the track widened by a couple of metres. It was an opportunity to sit down for a moment, get out of the wind. I leaned against the snow and took a deep breath. Then another. And another. This was not good. I was struggling.

'Dawa,' I said. 'Can you check my oxygen?'

He shuffled up to me and squinted down at the dial.

'You're at zero,' he said.

'All right, mate.' I wasn't surprised after all that delay. 'Grab me another canister.'

With that, Dawa's face dropped. He didn't need to say anything. Less than a second after the thought occurred to him, it occurred to me too. Of course. The Sherpa who was carrying all our extra canisters was with Ed, at least two hours away from us. I felt like a child. I needed help. But there was no help.

Here we were, at the edge of the Hillary Step and just above Everest's South Summit, less than a metre away from the body of the well-known expedition leader Scott Fischer, who'd died in 1996 in a situation just like this. I was weak. Freezing. My mind was going. Frostbite was setting in. And I had no oxygen. There was no fear bubble that was going to help me here. There was the sheer fact of reality. Would I join Scott Fischer on this ledge forever? No, I would not. If I was going, I was going in glory. I would jump off the mountain. Two steps that way and it was done. Over. I shifted my weight forwards and began looking for a place to kill myself.

As I was doing so, I saw Dawa had sprung away. What was he doing? I followed his progress. I realised he was remonstrating with the Sherpas who were just behind us, still assisting the man who'd held us all up. I checked myself. What was this situation? And what wasn't it? Right now, I was alive. I wasn't Scott Fischer yet. So what was I doing? I edged back into the crook of the ledge.

And then Dawa was coming back from his heated conversation, triumphantly holding a canister that contained five hours' worth of fresh oxygen. After he'd connected me up, I checked his level. He was on 50 per cent. We knew we had one canister stashed at the Balcony. This left us, in total, just enough to get to Camp IV, a long way off. We were still deep inside the death zone. There were no more chances. If we encountered any further problems, that would be it. For both of us.

The relief of Dawa's grabbing me this final lifeline was enough to get me on my legs. As I stood, I realised that I now had no feeling at all up as far as my ankles. I'd potentially lost both my feet. Fine. They were still mine for now. I would use those clumsy blocks to get me down.

Dawa and I began our descent as quickly as it was possible to move. Feeling as if I was strapped into a suit of concrete and pain, I pushed my way down through the storm, stumbling and slipping, clumsily picking my way past other gasping climbers. By now my focus had utterly narrowed. My mind was almost entirely free of thought. I was nothing more than a flesh machine, breathing in and breathing out, moving my arms, moving my legs, moving down the mountain inch by agonising inch, breath by ragged breath.

As we battled up above, Ed and the Madison team were below at Camp IV. They'd come to the conclusion that we were dead, and plans were being made to get a search team together to locate our bodies as soon as the storm had passed. But then, fifteen hours after leaving for the summit, Dawa and I finally emerged, stumbling into Camp IV.

'You're alive!' shouted Ed, when he saw us. 'I thought you were dead.'

'That was the most horrific thing I've ever witnessed in my life,' I said.

But I wasn't out of trouble yet. We were still thirty-six hours away from Camp II, the first place from which we could get rescued. I slowly cracked my frozen summit suit off and stuffed it down the bottom of my sleeping bag so it could dry out. After putting on my warm clothes, I tried to tell Ed how I was convinced my children would grow up without a father and how I'd just lived through the worst day of my life. But having breathed the canister oxygen for so long had left my throat dry and sore. I couldn't get the words out. Eventually, exhausted and still half-frozen, I fell asleep.

When I awoke at 5 a.m. I realised I couldn't see. I couldn't close one of my eyes. It felt as if it was filled with sand and I was getting nothing from it. From the other eye it was like looking out of smashed glass.

'That's where the snow's grazed your cornea,' said Ed. 'You need to patch it up. That stops your brain from trying to use it.'

He took out his first-aid kit and began covering my eye with a piece of cotton padding, strapping it on with lengths of yellow tape.

'I don't want to go down with you blind,' he said. 'It's difficult enough with two eyes. If you lose both it'll take us a week or so to get down.'

'I'm pretty beaten up,' I said. 'But my legs still work. I've got an eye. And I've got Ed.'

He grinned and put his arm around me.

'You're good at staying alive,' he said.

I rested my head happily on his shoulder. All our little tensions and differences of the past few weeks suddenly

317

seemed petty and ridiculous. In that moment I realised I had a friend and a brother for life.

WHEN WE FINALLY arrived back at Camp II I still couldn't feel my feet. And I wasn't sure if my vision would ever return.

'Are you going to call in a helicopter?' Ed asked. 'I think you should. You need treatment. We should get you to some medics as soon as possible.'

He had a good point. But how could I tell myself, in all honesty, that I'd passed the test of Everest if I hadn't come off it on my own two feet? How could that give me any pride?

'Fuck that,' I said. 'I'm going to walk.'

CHAPTER 14

THE OPPOSITE OF FEAR

DURING MY STRUGGLE down towards Camp II, the main thing on my mind, apart from the challenge of simply staying alive, was Emilie. She'd been expecting a phone call six hours after I'd spoken to her up on the summit. But as soon as I reached Camp IV and connected with Ed, I'd collapsed into sleep. Then I'd woken up and discovered I only had half an eye to work with due to my snow blindness. From that moment on, my single-minded goal needed to be to descend to the safe zone as quickly as possible. Phoning home would have to come later.

By the time we reached Camp II it was a full day and a half since Emilie and I had spoken. As we were approaching the now familiar spattering of tents and flags, I reached towards the pocket in which my satellite phone was stored. Ever watchful for dramatic action for his film, Ed immediately clocked what I was up to.

'If you're going to make a phone call, make sure I'm there to film it, all right?' he said.

I took my hand away. 'Yeah, yeah,' I said. 'Definitely. Let

me get some rest first, though. I need to get some ramen down me.'

You couldn't fault Ed. I knew my call with Emilie would make a nice scene for TV, but I really didn't want a camera in my face while I made it. I needed some space. I needed my wife. When I was sure Ed was safely out of the way, I located my two-man tent, crawled into it and zipped the door up behind me. For the first time in a long time I was alone, and it felt amazing. I slid the satellite phone out of my pocket and turned it on, hoping there was going to be some battery left. I'd lost track of both the time and the time difference between Nepal and the UK, and had no idea whether Emilie would be in or out. 'Please be in,' I muttered to myself as I entered our home number and listened to it ring. 'Please be in.'

'Hello?'

'Hi, Emilie.'

'You were meant to call me a day ago.'

'Yeah, sorry. Bit of bad weather. It's all fine now, though.'

It was a nice try, but she could tell from my voice that something was up.

'Ant, are you OK?' she said. 'Is everything all right?'

As soon as she said that, I burst out crying. There had been no internal warning that I was about to do so – no lump in my throat or heaviness beneath my eyes. It was the first time in my life I'd ever cried on the phone to my wife. Not even the relentless horror and terror of a war zone had done this to me. But I was just so relieved to still be there. I honestly thought I'd never hear Emilie's voice again. It was only in that moment that I allowed myself to believe I was going to see her once more. I realised how scared I'd been, and for how long. The adrenaline had finally drained away, leaving me sobbing like a child and having to explain to Emilie why I was so upset.

'I'm fine now,' I said, after pulling myself together. 'I'm safe now. But I nearly didn't make it down.'

'I knew something was wrong. I knew it when you were up there. I could tell. Where are you now? Are you still in one piece?'

'I'm not sure about my feet or my toes, and I can't see much. My eyes are shot. But don't worry, I'm going to get back down. We're in Camp II now, which is safety.'

'Is that where the helicopters land?'

'Yeah.'

'You should get airlifted out. Have you called one in?'

'I've already had this conversation with Ed. It's not going to happen. I'm walking.'

She started laughing.

'I'll give you a call when I'm at Base Camp,' I said. 'I love you.'

'I love you so much, Ant.'

'All right then ...'

'And Ant?'

'Yes, babes?'

'You're a fucking idiot.'

She was joking, of course. But also she wasn't joking. As I dried my tears and put my phone away, I found myself asking, 'Why do you have to do these things to yourself? What's wrong with you?' The only answer I could come up with at the time was, that was just me. It was who I was. I needed that buzz. I needed to be bursting those fear bubbles. I was addicted to them, and probably always would be. But at least I could safely say that, for the time being at least, the warrior ghost inside me had been tamed. I'd tested myself. I'd found that edge that made me feel so alive. And I'd survived, just. I've no doubt the day will come when I'll have to tame it all over again. But the next time, in the run-up, I might just go a bit easier on the chicken wings.

THE OPPOSITE OF FEAR

The fact that I'd cried openly and without holding myself back while on the phone to Emilie came as a surprise, suggesting that something had changed in me. I wasn't the man I'd once been. As I was pondering this, I was reminded of an incident that had taken place back home just before I left for Nepal. Every week my wife takes my three-year-old daughter to a local gymnastics group. There's a car workshop next door to it and the parking's divided between the two businesses. That day, Emilie had parked up in one of the

THE OPPOSITE OF FEAR

garage's spots by mistake. As soon as she'd got out of her car, the owner of the garage had come out to ask her to move it.

'I'm sorry,' she told him. 'I'm just dropping my daughter off. I'll move it straight away. I didn't realise.'

'No, no, no, can you move it now?' he said.

'I'm literally just dropping her off. I'll be two seconds.'

'You'd better move it now because I've got a garage here and you've got cars coming in and out,' he said. 'Unless you want me to run your kids over.'

Emilie was furious. She'd taken his comment at face value, as a threat to her children's lives. To say I was angry when I heard about it would be an understatement. If this had happened a couple of years ago he'd have been a dead man. But that afternoon I found myself doing little more than trying to calm Emilie down. I knew that nothing positive would come out of me paying him a visit. While what had happened obviously felt deeply personal – he was attacking my wife, threatening my kids – in actual fact it wasn't personal at all. It just happened to be Emilie who pulled up at that moment, and it just happened that he was a dickhead of a man who had a bee in his bonnet about parking.

So I didn't do anything. I let it go. If the old me could have looked into the future and seen all this, he wouldn't have believed it. 'That's not a man,' he'd say. 'A man would go in there and sort that idiot out. That's not me. There's no way I would act like that.' But today my reaction makes complete sense. For me, this is evidence that my life is going in the right direction. I'm learning. I'm growing. I'm constantly opening new doors and stepping into new corridors, and this is simply what happens when you do that. What is the opposite of fear? If you look in the dictionary you'll probably be informed that it's courage. But I believe that the true opposite of fear is growth.

My favourite quote of all time captures this idea perfectly. It comes from the philosopher Alan Watts, who once wrote, 'You're not something that's a result of the Big Bang. You're not something that's a sort of puppet on the end of the process. You are still the process.' For me, that process is personal growth. The universe is in a state of constant expansion, and you are part of that universe. It wants you to expand and change. If you learn to harness your fear and let it take you where it wants to take you, then positive change is inevitable. You'll become the person you never dreamed you were capable of becoming.

But it also takes guts. People will come up with all sorts of reasons to defend their lack of growth or even put the brakes on it. When people feel themselves changing, they sometimes worry that they're somehow not being 'true' to themselves, as if their identity is this dead thing that's inscribed in stone. But being true to yourself doesn't mean staying the same forever. It means taking what's already there and improving it. Think of it like a car. If you buy a bog-standard Ferrari, put a new exhaust on it, pump some different fuel into it, change the tyres and tweak the engine, it's still a Ferrari, it's still the same model that you bought from that dodgy guy in Ramsgate. But it now sounds different, it performs differently, it looks different, it even smells different. It's the same car, but it's changed.

It's true as well that human change can be particularly disorientating. When people grow, we often seem to become someone we never imagined we'd be. When Emilie had her falling out with the guy from the garage, I had the uncomfortable feeling of being negatively judged by an old version of myself. I heard his voice in my head saying, 'This is not a man.' It can be a powerful experience, causing you to pause and reassess. It can make you question yourself and your journey. But always remember, that judging voice inside is the manifestation of an inferior version of who you are now. They're in the past. They're dead. They're irrelevant. They're just another form of the negative chatter that the default mindset is always pulling out to keep you rooted in your place.

Sadly, it's not only dead versions of yourself that will want to judge you negatively for having the courage to change. People from your past will too. I hear from lads all the time who used to know me in the military and now see me on TV. It's usually not long before the loaded comments start. They say things like, 'You're not the same person who you were back then. If only they knew.' I know who I was back then. I was a fucking nightmare. I'm not that person now. I'm a civilian in a completely different headspace. And thank God for that. Can you imagine if I acted like that now? I wouldn't be in a job. I'd probably be in prison.

But people always want to define you by who they were when they first met you. They want to believe the 'true' you is the most basic, least evolved version of yourself. They often try to drag you back there. I always resist this pressure because I know that it's genuinely dangerous. I'm brutally honest about my weaknesses, and know what I need to do to stop myself from reverting to my old type and keep out of trouble. This is why I'm definitely not going out on some bender until 4 a.m. with a former soldier I knew twenty years ago just because he wants me to. So I politely and respectfully say no. And then I get the reaction: 'So you think you're better than me, then?' No, I don't. It's just that you want me to get wrecked and get into a fight simply so you can say, 'You see? This "new" Ant is all bullshit. It's fake. I told you he hasn't changed.' Then I think, 'Get your negativity away from me.' I want to be around growers, people who learn. And that's why my social circle has become smaller and smaller. It's not that I think I'm better than anyone else. It's not that I've become a 'fake' person. It's just that I'm changing. And hopefully, if you meet me again this time next year, I'll have changed all over again.

It seems to me that the main reason I make the negative few from my past so uncomfortable is that, by changing myself so much, I'm highlighting how little they've changed.

The learning, the graft and the setbacks I've been through just haven't been taken on by them. I might have been on their wavelength several years ago, but I'm not any more, and that offends them. It tells them something they don't want to hear.

Take my experience as a warning. If you follow the advice that I've laid out in this book, you too are going to change. Give it a few years and you might even find yourself unrecognisable to the person you are now. And then what will happen is this. Some of the people you know now are going to resent you for it. The more fear bubbles you step into and doors of opportunity you open, the more jealousy and resentment you'll attract. People who were once in the same place as you will believe they're owed what you've earned. They'll say, 'How come they've got that? They're the same as me. It's not fair.' They'll be offended that you've left them behind and will take your new success as an insult. They might say you're just putting your new self on and that you're fake. They'll reassure themselves that they know the 'real' you. They'll talk behind your back, feeding each other with negative chatter that reassures them that they were absolutely right to stay stuck in their safe corridors, because you've only changed for the worse.

Deal with these people in the only way the positive mindset allows. Kill them with even more success.

GODLIKE RESPONSIBILITY

Once you become well versed in using the fear bubble technique and begin growing as a person, you'll begin to notice some changes in the way you experience the world. As you keep on looking for new bubbles to burst, you'll start to feel a sense of extraordinary power growing within you. Now that fear has become an ally, rather than a terrible force you just want to run away from, you'll begin to feel as if you can tackle anything. And if you're following my technique with a healthily positive mindset, this feeling won't go to your head. You'll be motivated much more by pride than by ego, pushing on not because you want people to drown you in compliments but because you're simply enjoying the journey of testing yourself and seeing where the process can take you. If you pursue this, you'll ultimately enter a mindset of absolute personal responsibility. You'll feel like the god of your own fate and treat everything that happens to you as if you caused it.

And I do mean everything. Say, for example, you're coming home late from a club and you get beaten up down a dark alleyway. The normal and perfectly natural response to this would be to feel like a victim. And it's true, you are a victim. But what do you get out of interacting with reality in this way? Nothing but negativity. You're feeding that voice in your head that's determined to seek out and lock on to any sense of danger and threat. It doesn't matter what's true or not about that situation. Respond to it as if you caused it. What can you learn about what happened? Why were you down that dark alleyway at four in the morning in the first place? Why were you unable to fight off your attackers? What do you need to do to ensure nothing like that happens again? Forget whose 'fault' it was. Forget blame. That's just part of the victim mindset. It might not have been your fault, but make it your problem. Human beings are problem solvers, and now, as if by magic, you've got something to solve. You've got something to act upon in a positive way. This is how we grow and thrive.

Whatever badness happens to you, your conclusion should never be that the world just isn't fair. Even if that's true, it doesn't matter. You decide what's true. When I was serving with the Special Forces, I knew the truth was that I didn't have the ability to dodge bullets, but I decided to believe that I did. During firefights I acted with complete confidence, as if I had godlike control over what was happening to me. This lack of hesitation kept me alive. Other people I served alongside didn't have that mindset. They hesitated, and many of them ended up wounded or killed. I want you to start walking into rooms as if you can dodge bullets. I'm telling you, you can dodge bullets. It's possible. Don't believe me? I'm someone who has walked into rooms time and time and time again with AK47 bullets flying directly at me. I know that it's possible. It's simply a question of mindset.

CREATE YOUR OWN REALITY

Once you've adopted this mindset of godlike responsibility, you'll understand that you have the ability to create your own reality. Just as negative thoughts create a negative life, so positive thoughts create a positive life. Whenever I talk about this subject, I always remember a young man that I met when I was serving in Afghanistan. We'd just landed at a Forward Operating Base or 'FOB' in Helmand Province in order to refuel. FOBs are rough-and-ready bases that the military construct in war zones, often using what's left of bombed-out buildings. This was no exception. It was dusty and mostly open to the elements, and the hot desert sun beat down on its open spaces relentlessly.

There was a communal area in one corner made up of logs and cheap foldable chairs where the lads would gather round at night and play cards. Sitting on his own at one end was a guy who looked no older than nineteen. He was sobbing quietly.

'What's wrong, mate?' I asked him. 'What's up? Pull yourself together, yeah? Let's have a chat.'

'The next job we go out on it's my job to minesweep,' he said. 'It's tomorrow.'

'You've done minesweeping before, haven't you?' I said. 'You've survived it. Why are you crumbling now?'

'My best pal was doing it two days ago. He got blown up. It's my time next, right?'

'You cannot think like that,' I said. 'Your pal died honourably. And you've got to be rational about it. That means there's one less IED out there. And I doubt very much they're going to hit again so soon.'

'You don't know that, do you?'

'You're right,' I said. 'That's true. I don't know that. But you can't let this get to you. If you fail to get out of that door tomorrow morning, then someone else has got to take on your responsibility. You don't want to be putting them in the firing line.'

'So it's me in the firing line, then.'

It was pretty clear that I wasn't helping. Eventually, I left him to it. I felt bad for him. I just couldn't see how he was going to get out of that door the next day. I also felt strongly that his mindset was going to significantly increase the actual danger he was in. That kid was creating his own reality, and it was a bad one. His job as a minesweeper was to lead his men safely through territory in which explosive devices had been buried by the Taliban. With that kind of mindset, rather than finding a path through the danger, he was simply going to find the danger. He would be unconsciously looking for those mines. How we think defines how we act, and how we act defines the events of our life.

This is true for all of us. Say, for example, you have a boyfriend or girlfriend who has a negative mindset about you. They're a bit jealous, a bit paranoid, so they decide to look through your phone. I guarantee they'll find something. They'll zero in on the littlest thing and interpret it in that worst-case-scenario way. 'Who's this, then? Why has she given you kisses? And why did you give her a kiss back?' The world is full of information, both good and bad. We're surrounded by positivity and we're surrounded by negativity. It's your choice which set of information you spend your time focusing on. It's your choice whether you build yourself a reality that's populated by angels or by devils. Whatever you seek, I guarantee you will find.

Like that young man in that Afghanistan FOB, I also had to deal with plenty of shifts as a minesweeper. Easily my most dangerous mission was in the heart of Taliban-controlled territory. We were mounting an assault on a small town that was notorious as a hotbed of Taliban IED manufacturers. It was there that the electronics and the explosives met the technical experts, some of whom were among the most talented – and most feared – in the world. Put it like this. If you had to take your turn sweeping for mines, this was exactly the place you didn't want to do it. The honest truth is, I have no idea why I volunteered for the role. As soon as I raised my hand I thought, 'What the hell am I doing?' But when the night of the assault came, I put myself in that positive headspace. I had to find the path, not the obstacle. I had to have no doubt at all that I was going to live.

As I approached the outer limits of the location, I reached into my day-sack and took out my metal detector – a telescopic device with a foldaway head that I pulled at, clicking it into shape. Beneath my feet was dirt and gravel and the occasional shrub. As soon as the detector got within sniffing distance of the ground, it began picking up metal objects beneath the surface. I slowly and methodically began plotting a path through the electronic bleeps, planting a glow-stick behind me every thirty seconds so the lads could see the safe path I was finding for them. But the going was slow. It was extremely frustrating. All I wanted to do was get in there and get on with it. Before long I found myself thinking, 'Right, I've covered 150 metres, maybe more. Up until this point, I'm still alive. Everything is fine. I don't have a problem here.' I quickened my pace. Soon, I was going so fast that I was planting a glow-stick about every two minutes.

A voice crackled into the receiver in my ear. 'Fucking hell, Ant. Slow down, mate.'

I did as he asked, but quickly grew even more frustrated. I looked ahead. I still had about a mile to cover. Jesus Christ. The metal detector was going wild, *boop, boop, boop, boop-boopboopboop*. 'I've got this,' I thought. 'There's no problem here. I'm not going to go boom today.' Above the noise of the detector, there came a sudden sound like a million pieces of sand hitting the desert floor. What was it? I felt something on the back of my neck. Rain. 'This is bollocks,' I thought. Soon the rain began stinging my skin. It had turned into hail. A tiny ball of ice fell down the back of my shirt, then another one. 'I'm not having this,' I muttered. 'I've had enough. I'm not going boom today.' I stood up straight and began walking at a normal pace, across the IED-strewn dirt, straight towards the town. My metal detector was in meltdown: *bupbupbupbupbupbupbpbpbpbpbpbpbpbpbpbpb*. The noise of it only made me more determined. My pace got faster.

The radio buzzed again. The voice pleaded: 'Ant, fucking hell! What you playing at? Slow down!'

'No, there's no need,' I said. 'We're fine. Plus it's fucking hailing. You can get to fuck if you think I'm going to get wet. Let's just breach this place and get into some cover.'

I knew everyone was freaking out behind me, but I'd created my own reality. I'd decided I wasn't going to die and nor were any of them. And we didn't.

THE MISSION IS YOU

What is mission success? What exactly does that look like? When I was in the Special Forces, the idea of 'success' was tightly defined. As point man in a Hard Arrest Team, a typical mission that I led was successful if we arrested our target. But sometimes we'd get on location to find the target wasn't there. Does that mean our mission had failed? That all depends on your mindset. You can define success in any way you choose. Success could be catching the bad guys, or it could be me and my pals getting out of there alive. It could be me finding a mobile phone or a laptop that's going to get us into a terrorist network. It could simply be me continuing to learn how to become a better soldier, mission by challenging mission. There were plenty of operations that didn't go as we'd hoped or planned, but there were never any that I'd describe as a total bust. If you have a fully positive mindset, you can never really fail.

This is why tightly defining your life's mission, and judging yourself strictly on how close you're coming to achieving it, is a mistake. In particular, you don't want to define your primary mission as 'getting rich'. Success isn't money or cars or jewellery or a big house. I know millionaires who aren't happy. All the signs and signals from the outside world are telling them they're a 'success', but they're miserable. Cash is often something that comes as a result of success, but it can never be the mission itself. Human happiness is completely separate from material objects. Go back sixty years. Go back six hundred years. People were no less happy then than they are today, although they generally had much less. Wealth and bling are not directly related to well-being.

But whether it's cash or a particular job or some qualification, it's incredibly easy to get caught up in thinking the mission is some external thing. But the main mission – the one that you should never lose sight of – is you. As long as you're stepping into those fear bubbles and opening those doors, you're succeeding. Every experience you have fine tunes you a little bit more. It grows you. It's inevitable that such growth sometimes feels like failure. When things don't go as you'd planned, that negative chatter will kick in, telling you, 'I told you so. Don't ever do that again.' You might feel humiliated. You might feel bitterly disappointed. You're in the fire. It hurts. But that fire is forging a new you. No matter how it feels, it's not a moment of failure. It's a moment of change.

You know this, because when you ignore that chatter and go for it a second time, you'll find that you take on your challenge in a subtly different way. Your principal mission is not the little shiny prizes that you'll pick up along the way, it's simply to keep on growing. It's to overcome the power of that voice in your head that's calling you a failure. The reality is, it doesn't matter that you didn't win this contract or that race, or did or didn't get this or that job. None of these things negatively affects your main mission. The beauty of life is that you can't unlearn it. As long as you're changing, you're winning. You're part of that universal process.

You cannot fail the mission of you because that mission doesn't end until the very moment of your death. A well-lived life is like an Everest with no summit. You never get to the top of your mountain, and therein lies the joy. The summits that you're aiming for always turn out to be just ledges, bumps on the ridge. There's always another bit to climb. But whenever you reach those false summits, it's important to take the time to stop and enjoy the view. The other day a pal of mine said to me, 'I came home from work last night after a shit week and my two-year-old son, who'd been asleep, woke up and smiled at me. That smile made me feel like the king of the world. I realised that all the sacrifices I'd made to give my boy a safe home to live in and put food on his table had been worth it. All the anger I'd felt about my shit week instantly vanished.'

We don't acknowledge these moments enough. If the ultimate human fear is 'I shouldn't do this because I'm not good enough,' then there's also the opposite of that feeling, the one that my pal felt in that moment: 'This is exactly what I should be doing.' Moments like these don't come often enough, and when they do, it's important to sit on that ledge and breathe in the beautiful air. It's telling you that all the effort and pain has been worth it. This acknowledgement allows you to free yourself from negative feelings like resentment and regret and blame and anger that might have been building up. And, make no mistake, if you're experiencing these moments, you've earned them. You don't get them without pushing through fear. You don't get them without being brave.

These moments are waymarkers on your route to growth, reference points in life that tell you you're doing the right thing. They recalibrate you. They allow you to think, 'I'm glad all that sorrow happened, because look at me now.' All those moments in your past that felt so much like failure suddenly turn into success.

COMMIT TO GIVING YOUR LIFE TO YOURSELF

Your mission is you. As long as you're opening those doors, it's mission success. When I was in the military I vowed to give my life for my country. I want you to make the same commitment to yourself. Stand in front of a mirror, look yourself in the eye and make an oath: I will die in service of myself.

Putting yourself first isn't selfish. By giving your life to yourself, you become a better father, mother, brother, sister, soldier, employee. By taking godlike responsibility for your fate and creating a positive reality for yourself to operate in, you immediately begin to serve other people more effectively.

And nor is putting yourself first egotistical. It's about taking personal responsibility. It's about bettering who you are through self-reliance. It's about pride.

If you're truly willing to sacrifice your life for yourself, nothing will stand in your way. There will be no door you cannot open, no corridor you cannot reach. Living with fear as an ever-present enemy is a living death. It's time to put a harness on that fear. It's time to use it as an ally. It's time to step into that fear bubble and commit.

CHOMOLUNGMA'S LESSON

Seven days after leaving Base Camp for our summit bid, I finally got back, two stone lighter than when I'd first arrived. One of the curious things about doors of opportunity that appear in your life is that they so often arrive at just the right time to teach you just the right lesson. The door that led to Chomolungma was no exception. I recalled the night on which the idea presented itself to me, all those months ago. I'd been wined and dined and smothered in flattery in one of the world's most exclusive private members' clubs, recognised on the street and surreptitiously photographed on the tube. 'How are you enjoying your new life?' my barrister friend had asked me, before proposing a toast: 'To success!'

The problem with my 'new life' and its new definition of 'success', I now realised, was that it all seemed so perfectly designed to mess with a person's ego. Being on TV, performing on stage to sell-out crowds, writing a number one best-selling book – it was all a lot of fun but it made for an unhealthy environment that could so easily tip you into thinking you were something special. What else had happened that night? I'd decided that I wasn't going to take public transport any more. And the next thing I knew I was typing it into my phone: E.V.E.R.E.S.T.

Why did the king of the rocks call to me in that moment? What did that mighty mountain have to teach me? It did nothing less than pull down my trousers and spank me on the arse. It reminded me what success was. It dragged me up to its summit, battered me in snow and wind, then threw me back in my place. I'd been humbled. But as I packed up my gear at Base Camp and finally headed towards the helicopter landing pad for home, the only emotion that remained in me was pride.

ACKNOWLEDGEMENTS

THE EVEREST TRIP was a life-defining experience, but not one that I could have achieved without the team. Ed Wardle, a very strong and capable companion, kept me on my toes. Thanks for pushing me, buddy. And Dawa Lama, thank you for never leaving my side and living up to the legends of the Nepalese Sherpa.

And when it comes to bringing my story to life, there are two people I'd love to thank. First, the very talented Will Storr. The days and weeks we spent with each other have only made me more knowledgeable. You're the best in the business. And secondly, Jack Fogg, for his relentless dedication and for keeping me out of trouble.

It's all about the team and what a combination to have YMU and HarperCollins right by my side.

And lastly, forever and always, many thanks to my brothers Michael and Daniel, my uncle Andy, Julia and Philip, and never forgetting my extended family Mike, Michelle, Max and Elle Morris. I'm very lucky and fortunate to have you all in my inner circle. We haven't even started.